Y0-BVQ-789

# Balancing Principles
# for Teaching Elementary Reading

# Balancing Principles
# for Teaching Elementary Reading

**James V. Hoffman**
*The University of Texas at Austin*

**James F. Baumann**
*University of Georgia*

**Peter Afflerbach**
*The University of Maryland*

*With*

**Ann M. Duffy-Hester**
*University of North Carolina at Greensboro*

**Sarah J. McCarthey**
*The University of Illinois–Champaign-Urbana*

**Jennifer Moon Ro**
*University of Georgia*

LB
1573
·H459
2000
West

LAWRENCE ERLBAUM ASSOCIATES, PUBLISHERS
2000    Mahwah, New Jersey                London

Copyright © 2000 by Lawrence Erlbaum Associates, Inc.
All rights reserved. No part of this book may be repro-
duced in any form, by photostat, microfilm, retrieval
system, or any other means, without prior written per-
mission of the publisher.

Lawrence Erlbaum Associates, Inc., Publishers
10 Industrial Avenue
Mahwah, NJ 07430

Cover design by Kathryn Houghtaling Lacey

**Library of Congress Cataloging-in-Publication Data**

Hoffman, James V.
Balancing principles for teaching elementary reading /
James V. Hoffman, James F. Baumann, Peter Afflerbach, with
Ann M. Duffy-Hester, Sarah J. McCarthey, Jennifer Moon Ro.
        p.  cm.
    Includes bibliographical references and index.
    ISBN 0-8058-2912-1 (cloth : alk. paper) —
ISBN 0-8058-2913-X (pbk. : alk. paper)
    1. Reading (Elementary)   I. Baumann, James F.
II. Afflerbach, Peter.   III. Title.
    LB1573.H459   2000
    372.4 —dc21                                99-088957
                                                    CIP

Books published by Lawrence Erlbaum Associates are printed
on acid-free paper, and their bindings are chosen for strength
and durability.

Printed in the United States of America
10  9  8  7  6  5  4  3  2  1

# Contents

# Preface

The students in our schools are failing to learn to read, and poor teaching is at fault. Would you be surprised to read such a statement as a headline in the morning newspaper? Probably not. We write this book at a time when the crisis rhetoric about schools, teaching, and learning to read is extremely high. As educators, our instinctive reaction to this kind of criticism is to dig in our heels and loudly defend ourselves and our profession. Such a response does little to quiet the debate, nor do references to research documenting our growing successes in teaching reading serve to bring civility and reason to the discussion. We will never win this debate because this debate is not just about teaching reading. This debate has more to do with issues of power, control, economics, and politics than it does with reading pedagogy. But the reality is that we must continue to live and work in the context of this debate.

There are very real needs in our schools today. We are not as successful as we should be with literacy instruction in our work with minority children, children of poverty, and children for whom English is not a first language. However, let us not confuse this need with a general call for alarm and a portrayal of our

The work reported herein is a National Reading Research Project of the University of Georgia and University of Maryland. It was supported under the Educational Research and Development Centers Program (PR/AWARD NO. 117A20007) as administered by the Office of Educational Research and Improvement, U.S. Department of Education. The findings and the opinions expressed here do not necessarily reflect the position or policies of the National Reading Research Center, the Office of Educational Research and Improvement, or the U.S. Department of Education.

teaching and schools as failing. A crisis mode of thinking leads us to grasp for quick-fix solutions that are doomed to fail or, worse still, to have these kinds of nonsolutions imposed from above. The real challenges we face will take concentrated effort and time to resolve.

Crisis is not new to our profession. During the 1960s, Mary Austin and Coleman Morrison published a report of the findings from a comprehensive study of reading instruction in American schools entitled *The First R: The Harvard Report on Reading in Elementary Schools*.[1] This study drew on data gathered from a national survey of teachers and administrators, selected interviews, and site visits to hundreds of schools and classrooms. The evidence and interpretations offered by Austin and Morrison were highly critical of reading instruction in American schools, and added fuel to the already heated "great debate" surrounding teaching practices. They found, in contradiction to the claims that phonics instruction had been abandoned in schools, that typical reading instruction was highly rote, mechanical, and skill/drill based. Again and again, the authors lamented the absence of a research base to inform practice. They raised numerous questions regarding the quality of instruction in schools and made a plea for reform.

It is estimated that since the publication of their report, there have been over 25,000 research studies in the field of reading conducted and published in the professional literature (as compared with a total of 5,000 studies conducted in the 50 years prior to the publication of Austin and Morrison's book).[2] Although not all of these studies have focused directly on teaching and learning in the elementary grades, many have done so. As a result, our knowledge base has expanded enormously—enriched particularly by our studies of teaching and learning in real classrooms. Despite the controversies (e.g., whole language vs. phonics), distortions (e.g., "reading is just guessing"), and over-simplifications (e.g., phonemic awareness is the one sure key to success) that attract media attention, we have learned an enormous amount about effective reading instruction from this research.

Concerns over students' success in learning to read are as widespread today as they were in the 1950s, but these concerns are rooted in a changing reality. The "space race" and the threat of communism have all but disappeared as catalysts for change. The new challenges rise ironically out of our own progress. Our society's launch into the information age has increased demands for literacy and has created a whole new class of illiterates. The expectation for schools is no longer to simply raise levels of literacy performance for students to some minimum standard, but to anticipate and prepare students for the expanded demands of literacy in the world of the future.

There is a rising call within our profession for a balanced perspective on reading. We view the acrimonious debates over skills versus context, back-to-basics versus whole language, top–down versus bottom–up models of reading, as having accomplished little to advance our thinking or our teaching. We join in this call for balance. However, we caution against a view that the balance we seek can be described in terms of the quality and quantity of the instructional activities we offer. Balance is a concept that lies not in the instruction but within the reader. The instructional actions that support this balance differ for each student. Balancing principles underscore effective teaching practices. These principles serve to guide the teacher in setting goals, planning for instruction, and adapting to individual differences. The balancing principles we offer in this book are grounded in the most recent research in reading.

Our professional responsibility is clear. We must continue to focus attention on our students and the strategies that promote balance and not be distracted or deterred by the political debates that rage. We must continue to be planful, systematic, and reflective about our practices. We must continue to build professional communities (local networks, professional organizations) that link our inquiries together. We must continue to communicate with those outside the profession (our parents, the public) about who we are, what we do, and why we do what we do. We must accept accountability for good teaching, but never abdicate our personal responsibility for making good teaching decisions based on our professional knowledge and our knowledge of our students.

We, the authors of this book, are part of the professional community of reading educators. We work on a daily basis with teachers in classrooms, prospective teachers, clinicians, and tutors. Our goal is to represent what we have learned about effective teaching and learning to teach as members of this community. We write this book with four purposes in mind: (a) to offer a principled conception of reading and learning to read that is considerate of both the personal dimensions of literacy acquisition as well as the changes that are taking place in society; (b) to summarize the key findings from research that relate specifically to effective teaching practices; (c) to describe current practices in reading instruction with specific comparisons to the principles of effective practice identified in the previous section; and (d) to suggest an action agenda that is school-based and designed to promote positive changes in the quality of instruction.

These four purposes are reflected in the four-part structure of this book:
Part I: Our Professional Stance
Part II: Our Principles and Our Practices
Part III: Our Past and Our Present
Part IV: Our Plans and Our Future

We envision this book as a resource to be used in the building of a community of learners. We hope you will read this book with your professional colleagues—in a course of study, in a teacher/researcher book club, or in some type of in-service setting. Debate the ideas presented. Challenge our conceptions with your reality. Make sense within a community about what action is desirable. We offer some specific suggestions for strategies on how to do this in Part IV of the book, but caution you to not wait until then to explore the possibilities. Our goal is to present a text that offers a perspective for teaching that challenges us to think beyond labels of *whole language, literature-based, phonics,* and *balanced instruction*—a text that challenges us to think about

our underlying beliefs about teaching, and our shared commitment to making
schools more effective for the students we serve.

*—James V. Hoffman*
*—James F. Baumann*
*—Peter Afflerbach*

## NOTES

1. Austin, M. C., & Morrison, C., with Morrison, M. B., Sipay, E. R., Gutmann, A. R., Torrant, K.
   E., & Woodbury, C. A. (1963). *The First R: The Harvard report on reading in elementary
   schools*. New York: Macmillan.
2. Anders, P., Hoffman, J. V., & Duffy, G. (in press). Research in reading teacher education. In
   P. Mosenthal, R. Barr, M. Kamil, & P. Pearson (Eds.), *Handbook of reading research, Vol.
   III*. New York: Longman.

# I

# Our Professional Stance

James V. Hoffman
*The University of Texas at Austin*

*… nothing that has ever been written whether in verse or prose merits much serious attention.*

*… any serious student of serious realities will shrink from making truth the helpless object of men's ill-will by committing it to writing.*

Plato, Phaedrus (370 BC)

Literacy is a glorious discovery—for those societies and those individuals who have been fortunate enough to join the "literacy club." Plato may have been accurate in his assessment of the place of writing in the world of 300 BC, but his remarks are clearly out of line with the reality of today—so far out of line that they underscore the ever changing nature of literacy in our society. The third millennium promises even greater changes.

Literacy, in the context of the human development, is a relatively recent invention, barely 6,000 years old.[1] Cultures across time have evolved in their use of basic forms of writing systems (from pictographic to logographic and alphabetic representations) to achieve different purposes. They have evolved in their understanding and appreciation for the power of literacy to transform social and even cognitive processes. The discovery and refinement of alphabetic writing is recognized by many historians as a landmark development point. The evolution of literacy, however, did not end with the discovery of alphabetic writing systems. Literacy continues to unfold as reading and writing become an important part of the lives of increasing proportions of our society. Literacy also continues to unfold along with changes in the technology of reading and writing. Recent innovations in the electronic medium for writing, for example, cannot be regarded as simply a change in the form of transmission of written texts. The electronic medium is changing the ways in which we create, organize, and process texts. Although these electronic innovations into literacy are perhaps too current to inspect from an historical perspective, they must be a part of any consideration of literacy in the next millennium.

To describe the development of literacy and writing from a broad sociocultural perspective might suggest to some that the evolution of literacy has been equally distributed across all societies and all peoples. Nothing could be further from the truth. Control over the forms and uses of literacy has been, historically considered, an exercise in social control. The religious, the wealthy, the armed, have used literacy as a means to control access to information and knowledge. Challenges to the control over literacy by a privileged few have played an important part in societal transformations. The Protestant reformation, which took the responsibility for the interpretation of sacred texts from the hands of the church and placed it into the hands of the individual, is a landmark point in the evolution of literacy. The Common Schools movement that argued for universal, free, and compulsory education for all children in the United States is a landmark point in the evolution of literacy in the United States. The basic literacy initiatives in developing countries around the world mark a continuing point in the evolution of literacy. In all of these cases, and in many more, the privileged aspects of literacy have been challenged. Discrepancies in access to literacy remain as a part of our society today. Any look at the future of literacy in the next millennium must consider these discrepancies and the need to address them.

The development of literacy in each young child, while less auspicious than the movement of a society into literacy, is no less glorious an achievement. Consider the observations offered by these three preschool-aged children and the literacy understandings that underlie their comments:

(Puzzling over the restroom door signs in a department store, and spelling out loud) "M-E-N ... No, not me. W-O-M-E-N ... Oh shoot! There's men in there too!"

"That book's too hard for me. It has too many big words in it ... like (pointing to a word on the cover and saying) ... Dinosaur."

(While removing a thick Santa Claus-shaped note pad from her Christmas stocking) ... "This is great! You could use this for a diarrhea!"

These children are reading their world. They make sense, in their own way, of the signs society has placed before them. Their observations reveal the creative forces of knowledge, experience, and language interacting in a context of discovery. Children engage with print in a way that involves not just perception and cognition, but the total self that includes motivations, interests, beliefs, and values. Just as with oral language, the child's understanding and control over literacy processes grows in the context of goal-directed activity and a supportive environment.

Individual development and societal development of literacy come into complex interaction as the tools for literacy evolve. The young child who today manipulates text and graphics in a storytime software program is exploring the frontiers of literacy of the future. As the world changes, the reading of that world changes.

## THE READING PROCESS

Psychologists have puzzled over literacy processes and literacy acquisition for over a century, applying scientific principles of inquiry to one of the mind's most complex operations. The scientific study of reading has led to remarkable advances in our understanding. Just as print is more than just speech written down, so too reading is more than just the oral rendering of written text. Although the adoption of a simple view of reading as "the decoding of words" might appeal to those who prefer their goals neatly defined, the reality is that reading involves decoding and much more. Recently, psychologists have come to study learning to read in terms broader than a simple perceptual process. We find increasing numbers of researchers studying reading as the total investment of self in text. The term "engaged reading" has become a popular framework surrounding this line of inquiry.[2] This is a perspective we adopt whole-heartedly.

Engaged reading is conceptual, motivated, strategic, and social. The processes employed in engaged reading are complex and multifaceted. The independent reader (i.e., one who is self-sustaining, motivated, and successful) orchestrates a variety of skills and strategies to achieve success. What are the essential properties that characterize and enable independent reading? We argue that there are three broad dimensions to independence that serve to characterize what the reader does actively and well.

First, the independent reader *applies skills and strategies to access text*. When the reader applies knowledge of the alphabetic code to achieve rapid word identification, combines various word recognition skills and strategies to achieve fluency, and adapts reading strategies to reflect different goals and sensitivity to text features, he or she is demonstrating the necessary skills and strategies to access text. Second, the independent reader *seeks meaning through texts*. This seeking underlies the reader's motivation to engage with text. The reader may be seeking a virtual experience that evokes a pleasurable response, or the reader may be seeking guidance or direction through text, or the reader may be seeking new knowledge by engaging critically with the thoughts of others. And, the reader may be seeking some combination of the above purposes. Third, the independent reader *self-monitors reading*. The independent reader may reflect on the processes of engaged reading, on the products of reading experiences, and on his or her personal progress and development as a reader. We view these three dimensions as essential to independent reading, but this is not to say that the reader is always conscious of their importance or role. We argue that these dimensions are in evidence from the reader's earliest experiences with text, although their manifestations are qualitatively different along the path of development. The critical components of this conception are represented graphically in our model of the independent reader (see Fig. I.1).

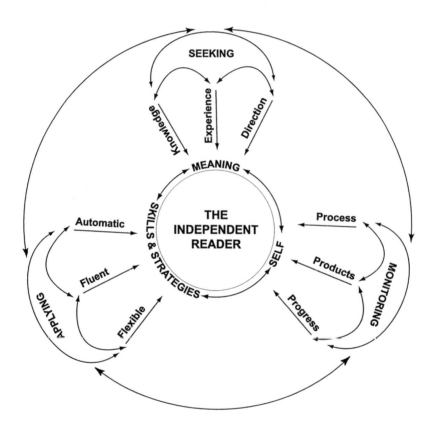

FIG. I.1.   A balanced model of the independent reader.

## READING DEVELOPMENT

We view the development of independence in reading as both a developmental and a social process that evolves over a lifetime of experiences with text. Control over the processes of reading is achieved in small steps. When viewed microscopically the steps may be so small as to be imperceptible to the learner. When viewed at the macro level, however, more defined patterns and points of growth become evident. We believe it is useful to view learning to read as evolving over a series of phases. We have adopted the term *phases* over *stages* because the former suggests less rigidity than the latter. These phases are not fixed points in development that can be specified by chronological age or any other simple system. We do not offer a phase perspective because it will help us classify, categorize, or otherwise label learners. Rather, we see a phase description of learning to read as helpful in revealing the various ways in which the learner is focusing his or her attention and energy at different points in time. The developing reader is skillful, seeking, and self-monitoring as he or she engages in reading regardless of the phase of development. Developing readers are refining their control over the skills and strategies associated with conventional reading. Developing readers are exploring and expanding the range of purposes for which they use text. And, developing readers are becoming increasingly reflective of their own development as literate individuals.

We have conceptualized the development process in terms of five phases:

1.   *Emergent*: From the time young children first contact print used in their environment, they are learning to read. The first days, weeks, months, and certainly, years of life are enormously influential on reading development. An early and vigorous launch into the world of language, both oral and written, sets the trajectory for growth. During the emergent stage the learner is focusing on print in the environment, books, features of the code such as the alphabet, and text structures such as narrative. The emergent period is also a time when learning oral language and written language interact. Learning about the script for written language (in particular in an alphabetic writing system like English) leads the learner to be more analytical about the structure of oral language. The learner begins to discover, for example, that the sounds of oral language can be segmented and manipulated in various ways that are outside of typical patterns of communication (e.g., deleting a sound, adding a sound, blending a sound).

2.   *Early*: Eventually children come to recognize some words outside of a specific environmental context. Typically, these words are highly familiar and important to the learner (the child's name, "Mom," "Dad," etc.). Words are recognized by their general shape or some aspect that cues the reader (e.g., the tail of the "y" on monkey). The reader has taken the first steps into conventional reading, but soon discovers that recognition by general configuration or visual cues is very taxing on long-term memory and not very efficient. The reader soon dis-

coverers that the letters, and associated sounds, are a helpful clue in reading not only familiar words, but even words the reader has never seen before in print. This personal discovery of the alphabetic principle is a major breakthrough point for the learner. There is no need to diminish this important landmark in development in order to advocate a developmental perspective. The realization of learning to read (the conscious reflection of gaining control over a process) is a notable accomplishment. Any primary-grade teacher can provide remarkable testimony to the power of this moment.

3.    *Fluency*: The learner brings to the process of learning to read an enormous amount of knowledge of language learned through oral interactions (e.g., knowledge of syntactical constraints of language, knowledge of the prosodic features of language, knowledge of meaning and pragmatics of language). There is abundant evidence that developing readers use this knowledge during the emergent stage. Research evidence also suggests that during the Early phase, as the reader engages in careful inspection of text features, the attention to surrounding support systems may be put on hold. During the integration stage the reader is not only growing more automatic in the use of alphabetic knowledge to decode words, he or she is also learning to utilize his or her knowledge of other language cue systems to achieve fluency in reading. The orchestrating and strategic use of cue systems is refined during this period.

4.    *Flexibility*: Ultimately, reading is a tool for us to use in learning and recreation. As the reader achieves higher and higher levels of automaticity and fluency, the opportunities for using reading as a "tool" become more accessible to the learner. The reader develops flexibility in adapting reading strategies to different purposes and different types of text. Texts have been a tool for learning and entertainment from the start, but it is at this stage that the reader assumes greater responsibility and control over the processes of active use. Reading is less an end now than it is a tool for growth.

5.    *Independent*: The independent reader is in control of the processes of reading. The independent reader is continuing to develop and refine his or her reading but not dependent on others for direct instruction. The independent reader has found a place for reading in his or her life that is fulfilling and liberating. The independent reader uses his or her knowledge, skills, and value system related to reading to achieve old purposes and discover new ones. The independent reader actively reflects on the use of reading as a tool, is aware and insightful about himself or herself as a reader, and is able to learn and grow from this kind of reflection.

We recognize the inherent controversies and difficulties with phase or stage models of development. We offer our conception as a "heuristic" model—one that helps us frame questions and organize understandings. We do not see the phases as lock-stepped or fixed in their progression. We see them as points in development where the developing reader's concerns tend to focus on certain areas. Exploration, experimentation, consolidation, and so on are all part of the process. We see no value at all in labeling a child in terms of his or her phase at a given point in time. We do see value in conceptualizing development in terms of continuous progression that evolves over time with varying points of growth and progress. The child's progress is influenced by the types of support that are provided within his or her social worlds.

## THE BALANCED READER

Piaget's writing in the area of intellectual development has been instructive to us regarding growth from a developmental perspective[3]. Intellectual development can be viewed, according to Piaget, as a process of expanding mental representations of the world as it is experienced by the learner. Mental models are creations that represent a "best-fit" explanation for these sensory experiences. As long as the existing mental models offer the learner a representation of reality that allows him or her to engage successfully with the surroundings, these models are used to assimilate new experiences. As the learner encounters novel experiences that cannot be explained by the current representations, a state of dissonance is introduced. The learner must adapt the mental structures in significant ways to accommodate new forms of information. The expanded mental model moves the learner to a new state of equilibrium with the sensory world.

We view the child acquiring literacy as expanding his or her mental operations, representations, and strategies as a particular case of Piaget's more general description of intellectual development. The developing reader is constantly challenged by an expanding reality of print in the environment. The developing reader is constantly adapting their representations and strategies to achieve success with these literacy events. These efforts to achieve a balance (or equilibrium) between the goals of the reader, the demands of the reading context, and the reader's abilities drive the development process. A good instructional program challenges the reader with new realities and opportunities for text experiences and provides the kind of supportive instruction that leads to immediate success and long-term growth.

In our model of reading we see the balance expressed in terms of the growing motivations of seeking meaning (the underlying catylist for change), the expansion of skills and strategies, and the increasing control over self-directed leaning that comes with monitoring performance.

## SUPPORTIVE CONTEXTS
## FOR DEVELOPING INDEPENDENCE

Learning to read, like the learning of most things, is social in nature. It is enhanced by observing others engaged in the process, experimenting first-hand with new skills and understandings, and receiving some systematic support from an expert or peer. Or in the vernacular, good modeling, a lot of muddling, and some timely meddling all contribute to sustained growth in reading.

Children are acquiring knowledge about all forms of communication that are used around them from the first point of contact. The child explores reading and writing in emergent, and in some cases conventional, forms long before entering school. These early forms of reading and writing are the first steps on the path toward mature use. They are nurtured in the context of the demonstrations of literacy events in the home, family and social institutions that are part of the child's life long before he or she enters formal schooling. The children who are offered these demonstrations on a frequent basis are not shy about stepping in to explore and interact with the processes. Parents, siblings, and other care-givers are there to offer support and guidance ("instruction") in how to engage the system successfully. They are there to provide responsive feedback and a safety net when the learner takes a risk and comes up short.

Is learning to read natural or unnatural? This is one of those dichotomies created by academics that serve no useful purpose for teachers but seem to fuel the frenzy of the public as they read the popular press accounts of dissension among educators. Such dichotomies divert our attention from the important questions we face. Learning to read is no more natural or unnatural than learning to talk. Literacy and oracy are social constructs that serve communicative functions. The acquisition of oracy skills is not a reflex action. It is not automatic, like breathing or a heart beat. The development of speaking and listening abilities depends on the availability of models, the opportunity to engage in meaningful use, and feedback. The same holds true for the development of literacy—both occur within social contexts. Is a family member available to read with a child? Are there books and writing materials in the home? Are expert users of reading and writing available to observe, offer feedback, and support the development process? Is a parent available to interact with a child in oral language? Is the context rich with vocabulary? Let the academics debate whether these are natural or unnatural features of the environment. The reality is clear—the richer the context, the richer the outcome.

## THE CHALLENGE FOR SCHOOLS

Elementary schools bear a major responsibility for teaching reading. To be effective, schools must be prepared to meet children who are already moving along the developmental path, recognizing that all children may not be at the same point at the same time. We must meet them not with a balanced program that offers a little bit of this and a little bit of that; we must meet them with a program that supports balance within the reader, and this may require very different strategies for different students. Our vision of balance in reading is not a new one to the field. Paul Witty[4] wrote over a half a century ago regarding balanced reading and the teacher's responsibility: " ... balanced reading instruction depends upon the teacher's understanding and knowledge of each child and his needs" (p. 2).

As educators, responsible for designing and delivering instruction in literacy, we must be prepared to offer the best instruction possible that is responsive and sensitive to a wide range of individual differences. Do classrooms meet our students where they are and yet challenge them to grow? Do the reading experiences we offer in our classrooms prepare them to read the world of today? Will the instruction we offer today prepare them to read and construct the texts of tomorrow? To answer these questions in the affirmative we must:

- Anchor our pedagogy in principles that can adapt to the changing reality for literacy in our society
- Anchor our pedagogy in principles that are derived from research, not "canned" program prescriptions or political directives
- Anchor our pedagogy in the belief that classroom teachers must assume responsibility for making the right decisions about good instruction for the learners they teach
- Anchor our pedagogy in coherent programs for instruction that provide the necessary support systems and organizational structures for teachers to be effective in serving all students.

These anchor points represent our professional stance. We must be articulate, reasoned, and practical in our representation of this stance to our students, to each other, as well as to the public. In the long run, we will change and adapt our stance as our inquiry and research lead us to new understandings. In the short term, though, we must enact a program of instruction that is based on our current level of understanding and uncertainty. What principles will guide us? How will our decisions be shaped? The answers to these questions are not to be found in a recipe for a balance of teaching activity and curriculum. The answers to these questions are to be found in a set of principles that are considerate of the needs of each learner as she strives to achieve balance in her literacy life.

## NOTES

1. Barton, D. (1994). *Literacy: An introduction to the ecology of written language*. Oxford, UK: Blackwell.
2. Guthrie, J. T., & Alvermann, D. E. (1999). *Engaged reading*. New York: Teachers College Press.
3. Piaget, J. (1952). *The constructions of reality in the child*. (M. Cook, Trans.). New York: Basic Books.
4. Witty, P. A. (1942). *The brave and free. Teachers manual* (p. 2). Boston: D.C. Heath and Company.

# II

# Our Principles and Our Practices

James V. Hoffman
*The University of Texas at Austin*

Sarah J. McCarthey
*The University of Illinois–Champaign-Urbana*

The engagement perspective for literacy challenges us to think differently about effective teaching practices in the elementary grades than has been the case in the past. The inherent complexity of an engaged view of reading (i.e., one that acknowledges its conceptual, motivational, strategic, and social dimensions) cannot be viewed through a narrow behavioral lens. Research into engaged literacy typically involves a variety of assessment strategies that tap not only the reader's thinking but the reader's motivations, strategies, and reflections as well. The social context for engagement is seen as a resource system for the reader to access and use. We offer a principled conception of effective instructional practices at the elementary level based on a synthesis of research that has assumed an engagement perspective for literacy.

## PRINCIPLED READING INSTRUCTION

The research evidence on what makes a difference for students in learning to read is clear. It is not the method or the materials. It is the teacher and the quality of teaching offered. Methods and materials are resources for effective teachers, but they do not determine teacher actions. How these materials and methods are combined and orchestrated is the product of teacher planning and decision making. Teachers who make a difference in student learning operate from a basic set of understandings in making these plans. These teachers are:

1. Knowledgeable about the functions of literacy, the processes of literacy, and the development of literacy,
2. Skilled in the use of a variety of tools and strategies for inspecting individual abilities and needs,
3. Instructionally responsive to the range of individual differences in their classroom by drawing on a wide variety of strategies, materials, and methods, and
4. Reflective about their own teaching and teaching processes in a way that supports expanding professional expertise.

We refer to teachers who possess these characteristics as "principled." A principled teacher is guided in his or her actions by these four basic understandings. Walk into any classroom and observe a teacher engaged in reading instruction. Although you might have some sense of the quality of the teaching based on the students" responses and the nature of the interactions you see and hear, the quality of the teaching is best revealed through a focused debriefing. Talk with the teacher after the observation regarding instructional actions:

- Why were you teaching this lesson?
- What were you thinking as the lesson was going on?
- What adjustments did you make to your plan and why?
- What did the students learn?
- What did you learn about your students?
- What lesson will come next?

The effective teacher tends to respond to these kinds of questions in terms of the four basic understandings we have outlined. His or her actions are principled in the sense that they can be traced back to a focus on the learner and the needs of the learner. Less effective teachers tend to respond in terms of curriculum or program demands (e.g., "It's what we are suppose to teach." "It's the next lesson in the book." "It's what our grade level team agreed to teach this week.") or other external constraints (e.g., "I need to get the students ready for the test.").

In organizing Part II, we have derived nine principles of effective teaching that guide practice. The nine principles are nested within our model of the independent reader's abilities and motivations to apply skills and strategies to access text, to seek meaning through texts, and to self-monitor reading activity. The nine principles do not describe balanced reading instruction. They describe the action points for the teacher to support the reader toward balance. The value of the nine instructional principles comes in the attention they bring to specific kinds of tools and activity structures that appear essential in supporting the developing readers growth toward independence. The specific principles suggest standards for success and apply across the literacy program. Within each of the areas, we describe the challenges that the engagement perspective brings to the teaching of reading in contrast to traditional forms of instruction. Our goal is to be illustrative in describing the principles not exhaustive of the instructional possibilities associated with an engagement perspective.

## INDEPENDENT READERS APPLY SKILLS AND STRATEGIES TO ACCESS TEXT

The teaching of the basics in reading has been the subject of much discussion and some heated debates in both the public and the professional media. It is true that some children do learn to read (and this includes learning to decode) without formal instruction. It is also true that direct, explicit instruction in reading skills that is offered in the context of meaningful language experiences helps many children learn to read with greater ease. And it is true that a large number of children will fail in their attempts to learn to read if they do not receive direct, explicit instruction in skills.

Skilled and strategic reading involve (a) automatic decoding processes for word recognition, (b) fluency in the reading of connected texts, and (c) flexibility in adapting strategies to purposes and text characteristics. We concentrate our first three instructional principles to the goal of developing the skills and strategies that support the developing reader's ability to access texts.

## INDEPENDENT READERS ARE AUTOMATIC IN WORD RECOGNITION

**Instructional Principle 1: Effective reading instruction focuses students' attention on print, in rich meaningful contexts, with the specific purpose of nurturing skills and strategies in word identification (see Fig. II.1).**

There is no question that in learning to read an alphabetic language like English, the developing reader must learn to decode words. The decoding process, at least at the early stages, is mediated by a phonological mapping of letters or letter chunks with associated sounds. There is no great debate over this assertion in the minds of most literacy researchers or classroom practitioners. There is, however, a substantial and continuing debate as to the best way to support this learning. Our review of the research in this area suggests no compelling evidence that traditional, synthetic phonics programs are particularly effective in achieving this goal. The calls for a return to the basics of the past taking the form of isolated skill and drill instruction followed by endless phonics worksheets are not, despite claims, supported by any body of scientific evidence. The research literature does suggest some of the features of programs and teaching that are supportive of students learning to decode.

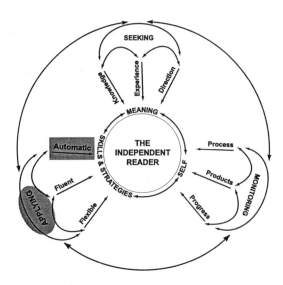

FIG. II.1.    The independent reader applying skills and strategies of automatic reading.

We offer a description of six features of effective decoding instruction. These features are described in the context of one first-grade teacher's classroom, Pam Stillwell, who has been widely recognized as an effective teacher of the language arts. Pam was a participant in a longitudinal study of first-grade reading instruction supported by the National Reading Research Center.[1] The features we describe from her program find strong support in the research literature on effective code instruction in beginning reading.

Effective code instruction in beginning reading is:

1.  *Pervasive*: During one of our early interviews with Pam, we asked her to describe her reading time. She rolled her eyes in response to our query. She proposed that we come and observe for a day and then we could tell her when her reading time was. Pam's language arts instruction is integrated across all forms of language use (reading, writing, listening, and speaking) and content (social studies, mathematics, science, literature). She divides her day in terms of activity structures (e.g., morning message, warm-ups with poetry, old favorites, inquiry) and within each activity structure all forms of language are nurtured. Trying to pin down Pam to talk about when she teaches decoding in her reading program is just about as difficult as pinning down her reading time in the instructional day. Pam tends to talk about her plan for teaching decoding more often in terms of children's writing than in their reading. Invented spelling is encouraged. Code

knowledge, she believes, is much more functional, early on, for students in their attempts to write than in their attempts to read. The skills and associations learned through writing will become useful strategies in reading as acquisition progresses. Language play (e.g., rhyming, segmentation, word games) are taught in the context of experiences with poetry. The ear is trained as well as the eye to notice patterns in language. Pam's teaching illustrates for us that effective instruction in decoding must cut across not only literacy but also oracy skills at the same time. The breakthrough to phonemic awareness is locked not just in oral language but in the interaction of oral and written language.

Talk about the code and how the writing system works is pervasive and connected across these contexts. Interactions focused on code are as likely to occur in the Inquiry time as in the Warm-Up time. Pam is constantly challenging students to look for the patterns in print, to describe what they see, to explain how the author has used print to communicate to the reader (or, in the case of writing how the student will use the code to reach his or her readers). Pam is constantly asking students why an author might do something in a particular way with print (e.g., use of an exclamation point), and when they might use this convention themselves as writers.

2. *Systematic*: We use the term *systematic* here to refer to teaching that is planful and targeted toward specific, a-prior learning outcomes. Pam enters into each instructional day, into each instructional activity with very focused objectives in mind. Pam structures the daily tasks (e.g., the selection of materials, the independent work to be done) within activity structures to reflect the goals they have set. The full depth of Pam's planning toward specific objectives was revealed only through our conversations with her. The talk about code on a given day in Pam's class will range over a broad number of issues—so many, so often, and so connected to the students observations—that it appears to be totally spontaneous. The fact is, that in every activity Pam has targeted specific code related objectives for her teaching. These elements are very specific (e.g., short o, /ch/ digraph, the -oon phonogram). She has selected the texts to lead to a focus on these elements. She relentlessly guides students to notice these elements. She plans for extensions that will require students to use these elements in their own work. On those occasions when we have interviewed Pam before an observation and had her talk about her goals for the day, we see the patterns in her teaching. Without prior knowledge, it is difficult for the outside observer to notice the targeted objectives from all those that are talked about and worked on that day.

"How do you select your objectives for each day?" Experience is Pam's short answer to this question. After years of teaching young children, she knows what they are learning about and the kinds of focus points that will nudge them along in their development. She, like most first-grade teachers, recognizes a special responsibility in teaching her students about the alphabetic principle and how it works to support reading and writing. She does not assume a "kids learn to read in first grade" attitude. She recognizes that much has gone on before and much will go on after her students leave. But developmentally, it is code that most of her first-grade students are working to understand. Of course, this broad knowledge of development provides only a general framework for planning. Each student and each group of students are different in their needs. Pam shapes her teaching objectives to the needs of students.

We would point out that Pam's systematic teaching is not rigid in any sense. There is no prescribed sequence of skills to be taught, no notion of the need to master a particular skill before moving on to another. The system Pam follows is more complex and reflects the dynamic properties of the literacy acquisition process. Nor does Pam's system blind her to teachable moments. Pam is opportunistic in her teaching. She is constantly challenging students to look for patterns in words. She builds on these discoveries with mini-lessons that not only support but extend the students' discoveries.

3. *Explicit*: Pam's talk with her students about code is explicit. The traditional boundaries set on phonics instruction in an "analytic" mode preclude the isolation of sounds. The search for patterns using an analytic approach to phonics typically stops before you reach the level of sounds isolated from words. Thus, the tradition is that you can say: "Bird begins with the same sound as you hear at the beginning of boy;" but you cannot say: "Bird begins with the /B/ sound." As far as we can tell, Pam breaks all of the rules.

To illustrate Pam's explicitness in dealing with code, we offer the following exchange that occurred during one of Pam's morning message lessons:

| | |
|---|---|
| Pam and Students: | I was at a meeting. |
| Pam: | Good, can you help me spell meeting? /m/(writes m) /e/. |
| Students: | e, e |
| Pam: | Two Es good. Meet-/ing/ |
| Students: | i-n-g |
| Pam: | I was at a meeting. Good. Period. New sentence. |
| Pam and Students: | I learned a lot of things. |
| Pam: | Let's see if we can spell things. Chris? |
| Chris: | F |
| Pam: | You think an F. Let me show you. Look at my mouth. Th-ings. Like in Thursday. See how my tongue kind of goes up. Th-ings. If it were an F, it would be /f/ ings. See how my mouth looks different. Anybody know what 'things' begins with? |

Pam isolates sounds, stretches sounds, blends sounds, and connects sounds with letters in ways that support the students' discovery of how the oral code maps onto the written code.

4. *Strategic*: Pam is not only explicit about how the code works, she is explicit about how this knowledge can be useful to the developing reader and

writer. She explains how and when this code knowledge can be used when students are engaged on their own as readers and writers.

Pam monitors and reinforces the use of these strategies as students engage in their independent work. She is quick to remind students to activate their knowledge of the code and to apply it strategically to solve the puzzles they face (e.g., decoding a word, spelling a word). Eavesdropping on student talk during writing in Pam's classroom, we heard the same terms and phrases used by the students to talk about strategies for encoding as we had heard Pam use in her teaching.

| | |
|---|---|
| Pam: | Belle, can you read your journal entry to me? |
| Belle: | (reading aloud from her journal): Today I learned about ducks for my project work. I learned that ducks have soft feathers, and water-proof feathers … |
| Pam: | I notice that you have periods at the end of you sentences. Tell me how you knew to spell feathers f-e-a-t-h-e-r-s? |
| Belle: | At first I had a f-e-t-h, but Alex reminded me that sometimes /e/ is spelled with two letters like our warm-up today about the sleepy head. |
| Pam: | Did he spell it for you? That was nice Alex. |
| Belle: | Nope, he just said remember that sometimes /e/ is spelled like in head. |
| Alex: | I remembered because I'm the "background knowledge king." |
| Pam: | You are the "background knowledge king." |

Pam's goal is to get the students to see the patterns, to understand how the knowledge of conventions can be used to help readers construct the author's message, and how they can use this knowledge strategically in their personal writing.

5. *Public*: There is an old axiom in teaching that relates to making the private public. Most of what we do in skilled reading goes on inside the head. A skillful teacher works hard to make these internal processes visible to the learner. Pam makes the decoding process visible to her students, in part, through her explicit talk. In addition, Pam makes visual displays of text in the classroom that support the talk about code. Word walls with phonogram patterns are integrated into the instructional plan for decoding. Students are encouraged to use these word walls as support for their decoding of difficult words and for the spelling of words in their writing.

Pam makes use of charts in teaching about the code. The warm-ups for poetry are studied for phonic elements and patterns. These charts are laminated and the students work with the teacher to mark the patterns that are noticed. Similarly, the overhead is used in constructing the morning message with the students. This interactive writing event combines both the explicit talk about the code along with the visual display of patterns and sounds.

Public displays are found in the Pam's word card collection and the students' word banks. These are used for word sort activities in which common phonetic, structural, and syllabic patterns are analyzed. Finally, public displays are achieved through the use of sound and letter boxes following the El Konin and Reading Recovery strategies for sounding, encoding, and blending.

6. *Diagnostic*: Pam is well-versed in the area of performance assessment. Rather than fearing assessment, Pam welcomes it as an ally in her teaching. She has become highly systematic in the ways in which she documents, records, and interprets student learning. She uses the data she collects as a resource for her planning, for her communication with parents and other teachers about student progress, and as a tool to engage her students in self-reflective evaluation. Students are becoming involved in setting personal learning goals and in documenting progress toward these goals. They speak freely about their strengths and weaknesses, about the strategies they employ, and about their growing awareness of themselves as learners. They recognize their ownership over tasks and projects and comment about the importance of their control over their learning. Given that these students are first graders it is an amazing process to observe.

## IT'S THE TEACHING THAT MAKES THE DIFFERENCE

Pam's teaching is illustrative of six features of effective code instruction. These features are widely utilized by effective teachers across the country. The features, as we have described them, are not bound within a packaged program. They are the essential elements of good code-focused instruction that can be used across various programs for teaching reading. Studies of highly effective teachers suggest that these elements of good code instruction are shared widely. Highly successful programs that have strong decoding components, such as Irene Gaskin's Benchmark Program[2] and Pat Cunningham's "Making Words" strategy,[3] emphasize similar aspects of teaching.

The research literature on the development of decoding suggests two cautionary notes: First, an extreme focus on decoding to the exclusion of a focus on comprehension and motivation does not support the development of good reading habits. Reading is a complex process and efforts to over-simplify and over-compartmentalize the learning are doomed to fail. Vocabulary development, comprehension, and motivation can and should be addressed along with decoding in a simultaneous, complementary, and balanced manner. Second, attempts to restrict texts to words that are highly decodable and contain the elements that have been taught in a phonics program are detrimental to the development of strategic reading, fluent reading, comprehension, and motivation. There is no evidence that such texts accelerate in any way the discovery of the alphabetic principle. There are abundant opportunities to develop and apply code knowledge in texts that reflect the inherent complexity of

English orthography. These texts offer opportunities for students to infer the more complex relationships in our orthography that occur at the morphological level as well as encourage the orchestration of word recognition strategies to complement and support phonological processing.

## INDEPENDENT READERS ARE FLUENT IN PROCESSING TEXT

**Instructional Principle 2: Effective reading instruction provides ample opportunities for students to engage successfully with connected text in ways that encourage the development of *skilled and fluent* reading (see Fig. II.2).**

Skilled readers know much more about the written text than just how to decode words. Developing readers brings with them a wealth of linguistic knowledge and draw on this knowledge in learning to read. Developing readers already know about the syntactical structures and constraints present in any language through their oral language experiences. This knowledge provides an enormous support system for learning to read. Developing readers also know about the communicative intent that is part of language use through their oral language experiences. This expectation provides another enormous semantic support system for sense-making while reading. The challenge in reading "connected" text is the orchestration of the reader's developing knowledge about the code with the existing and expanding knowledge of syntax and semantics. Readers who are able to move beyond the discovery of the alphabetic

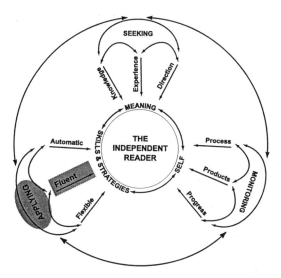

FIG. II.2. The independent reader applying skills and strategies of fluent reading.

code to fluent reading are the readers who learn to be facile in the use of all of the cue systems available.

The development of fluency is manifested most directly in oral reading performance. The accuracy and rate of reading reveal something of the level of successful coordination and use of the cue systems by the reader. A qualitative analysis of the patterns in miscues is an additional source of information about the learner's reliance on the various cue systems as he or she attempts to construct meaning. The development of fluency is also manifested as the reader begins to interpret text orally in a manner that reflects natural expression. The phrasing patterns, the points of word emphasis, the rising and falling pitch often suggest a deep level of processing on the part of the reader. Although less visible, the development of fluency is an important feature of silent reading as well. The developing reader eventually discovers that the oral production of text (that was perhaps supportive in the development of basic decoding abilities) is limiting the efficient processing of text. For many students this breakthrough occurs at around the third-grade level, but for some students it can occur much earlier.

Can we teach fluency? The research evidence is clear that we can. Despite the fact that we can, most teachers do not offer any focused instruction in fluency. In fact, some recommended instructional practices (e.g., always having student practice in material that is written at their instructional level) may inhibit the development of fluent reading. Richard Allington has described fluency as the neglected goal in reading instruction.[4] Although fluency, like code knowledge, may develop "naturally" for many children through wide reading, it is important to realize that there are specific activity structures that can enhance growth for those who require additional support and guidance. Stahl, Heubach, and Crammond have proposed an instructional model for fluency instruction using an engagement perspective that incorporates many findings from research.[5] Their approach is based on five goals and is directed toward the development of fluency among primary-age students. These goals are:

- *Lessons are comprehension-oriented even when smooth and fluent oral reading is being emphasized.* This is important, they argued, because students need to be aware that the purpose of reading is constructing meaning, and that the practice they are undertaking will make them better comprehenders of text, not simply better word callers.
- *Children read material at their instructional level.* Based on the findings from their research, Stahl and Heubach raised questions regarding traditionally accepted standards for determining instructional level (i.e., 95%–98% accuracy). They argued that practice in text that is more challenging contributes to the development of fluency if there is sufficient instructional support offered.
- *Children should be supported in their reading through repeated readings.* This was found to be a critically important part of the fluency building model. There were varying forms of support offered to stu-

dents as contexts for the repeated reading of texts including echo reading, home reading, choral reading, and so on. The amount and form of the support offered should vary in relation to the readers developing control over the text.

- *Children engage in partner reading.* Partner reading is a context for support that proved to be particularly effective in promoting fluency. Partner reading provides an opportunity for students to read connected text within a socially supportive context. Partner reading provides an effective alternative to round-robin reading and offers extended opportunities for engagement. Partner reading also provides the teacher with an opportunity to engage in monitoring student progress.

- *Children increase the amount of reading that they do at home as well as at school.* Even small differences in the amount of home reading practice have been shown to have a significant effect on growth in reading ability. Within this goal, Stahl and Heubach identified several strategies for increasing time spent in reading in school and at home. For home reading they encouraged the rereading of basal stories read at school and the reading of tradebooks from a "take-home" library. For in-school reading they encouraged increased use of choice reading time during the instructional day.

Stahl and Heubach worked with classroom teachers to revise their current classroom routines toward a model that stresses the development of fluency. They worked with teachers to revise the traditional basal reading lessons from a more traditional Directed Reading Activity (DRA) format to a model that combines elements of shared reading, partner reading, and free-choice reading. The evaluation of the results of this model suggest that a fluency-oriented model of instruction produces significant positive effects not only on fluency but also on word recognition, comprehension, attitude toward reading, and students' view of themselves as readers.

Although some argue against instructional models that encourage the development of fluent reading through direct modeling, repeated practice, and partner reading because they are too behavioral in focus, research conducted within the engagement perspective suggests that such models can become highly motivating. Shared reading that emphasizes expression and interpretation is highly engaging to students. This is particularly the case when the text offers rich and interesting language. Many children's authors (e.g., Dr. Seuss) and literacy educators (e.g., Bill Martin, Jr.) have provided us with demonstrations of texts and contexts that support the development of fluency. Stories that are highly predictable and filled with rhyme, rhythm, and humor provide a rich and motivating context for growth.

The development of fluency is a particularly troubling and challenging aspect of literacy acquisition for the student who speaks English as a second language. These students bring to the task of learning to read limited knowledge of rhythms of the English language and its syntax. In contrast to students who speak English as a first language and find they can use their knowledge of the structure as a support for success, students who speak English as a second language may experience interference in the acquisition of fluency. When instruction in the student's first language is impossible, it is imperative that direct instruction in fluency be offered. Irene Blum and her colleagues have demonstrated the benefits of using books to extend literacy instruction into the homes of second-language learners.[6] Books that had been shared with the students in school as part of the instructional plan were audio-taped and sent home with the students for repeated and extended practice. Parental training and support were offered. The results indicate substantial benefit from the opportunity to practice books with audio tapes at home. The support provided by the audio tapes enabled students to fluently read increasingly more difficult texts. Also of interest was the positive effect on these students' reading motivation and behaviors.

One further consideration in the development of fluency is student practice in relatively easy text. Research suggests that student practice in text that presents minimal challenge in terms of decoding, may be a rich context for building fluency. Jim Guszak argued that a regular time each day for students to practice in text written at their independent level (98%+ accuracy) is crucial to building fluency.[7] "Build-up" readers (or texts that are constructed from high frequency, highly familiar, and highly decodable words) may be useful for bridging success into higher levels of decoding ability as well as building fluency.

The key to the transition to silent reading fluency from oral fluency appears to be quite simple: practice. The more students read, the more fluent they become. The more fluent students become, the more they read. The only specific research finding regarding the movement from oral to silent fluency is that specific strategies designed to discourage the oral reading of text in favor of silent reading may have negative consequences. Subvocalization that accompanies silent reading suggests that the reader is still struggling in some way with decoding or orchestrating the cue systems. Attempts to directly discourage subvocalization are misguided and doomed to fail. The more appropriate focus is on the student's basic decoding and word recognition abilities in relation to the demands of the text. Find easier text for practice.

Help for teachers in the selection of texts that are appropriate for the development of fluency is growing as more valid leveling systems for texts have been developed. It is clear that traditional readability formulas provide little help to teachers in making decisions about appropriate text for the beginning reader. Such formulas consider a very limited number of features, relying mainly on word difficulty and sentence complexity measures. They do not consider all of the other possible forms of support possible in texts designed for beginning readers. In our haste to throw out the readability formulas, we may have overlooked the need to provide texts that offer students a place for successful practice. Recent developments in strategies for text leveling suggest consideration of such factors as: (a) picture support, (b) patterns in rhyme and rhythm, (c) familiar concepts, stories, and poems, (d) cumulative stories, (e) repeated phrases and patterns.

In recent years, leveling systems, such as those proposed in the Reading Recovery model, offer a framework for laying out a wider distribution of levels of supportive texts. This wider distribution of text levels and support allow us to make better matches between the reader and text to build fluency.[8] We now have text structures available that make it possible for every child to be successful as a reader and at the same time challenge him or her toward higher levels of proficiency.

The use of such systems to select texts for students must be moderated by the teacher's careful monitoring of performance. Through the use of such assessment strategies as Informal Reading Inventories, Miscue Analysis, and Running Records the teacher can monitor text appropriateness for the goal of nurturing fluency. Too difficult a text will not provide a useful context for building fluency. The careful monitoring of performance must focus not just on word accuracy and rate as the important indices of processing, but also on fluency itself. We recommend that the teacher apply the following scale as a simple guide in rating the reader's fluency during the oral reading of texts:

1 = Slow, laborious, choppy, word-by-word reading,

2 = Some attention to phrasing and grouping of words,

3 = Appropriate phrasing for most of the text, reads with some intonation and word emphasis,

4 = Good phrasing and intonation for almost all of the text,

5 = Expressive, interpretive reading.

This kind of rubric for fluency can provide a useful guideline for teachers and students in setting goals and evaluating growth in this important area.

## INDEPENDENT READERS ARE FLEXIBLE IN ADAPTING TO PURPOSE AND TEXT STRUCTURE

**Instructional Principle 3: Effective reading instruction encourages students to become *skilled* and *strategic* in ways to adapt their reading to their purposes and to text characteristics (see Fig. II.3).**

Flexibility, as a characteristic of skilled reading, is a concept filled with misconceptions. Three misconception stand out. The first is tied to a limited image of the engaged reader. For many of us, the image of the engaged reader is something like the adult relaxing in an easy chair with a book, or a child snuggled in bed reading by a flashlight. Although these are viable images of engaged reading, they are tied primarily to recreational or pleasure kinds of reading experiences. In fact, the engaged reader uses many different types of texts for many different purposes. Automaticity in decoding and fluency are a part of all these types of reading experiences, but the actual task demands for the reader may be quite different as a function of the text and context. The reader working with

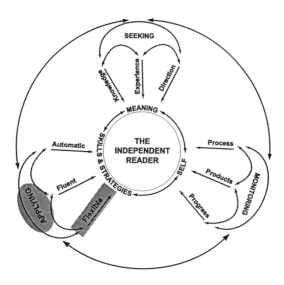

FIG. II.3.   The independent reader applying skills and strategies of flexible reading.

a hyper-card text program on a computer, the reader using an encyclopedia to locate a specific piece of information, the reader scanning the sports page to find a favorite team's box score, and the reader studying a chapter in a physics text using a study guide to get ready for the next day's test are all engaged with text. These are very different kinds of tasks, however, and underlying each is a distinct set of behaviors, understandings, and strategies that enable the reader to achieve success.

A second major misconception in this area is that flexible readers adjust their rate of reading to difficulty of the text and their purpose for reading. In this view, the flexible reader slows down when the text gets difficult and/or the purpose is to "study" the content; and the flexible reader speeds up when the text gets easy and/or the purpose is to just get the general idea. This, again, is a flawed notion. The flexible reader is one who is skilled at adjusting his or her reading strategies in consideration of his or her purposes for reading and the structure of the text. The flexible reader reflects on her purpose for reading, assesses the text structure, and then selects the appropriate reading strategies or combination of strategies. The reader may skim, scan, study, or "read" every word or employ some combination of these. As Ron Carver has demonstrated repeatedly, the notion that somehow the speed of reading is adjusted to reflect task demand is at least inefficient, if not impossible. [9]

A third major misconception in this area has to do with an old adage that first you must "learn to read" (this occurs in the primary grades) and then you "read to learn" (this type of reading begins in earnest in the intermediate grades). Following this misconception, reading instruction in the elementary school, particularly in the primary grades, has tended to use narrative texts as the primary vehicle for practice. Narratives are seen as somehow inherently motivating and therefore offer an easy transition for the language learner from the oral narratives of early childhood into early reading. In this context of narrative, the developing reader learns the strategies to process all kinds of texts. However, if narrative is the exclusive diet, then the strategies associated with flexible reading may not be nurtured. There is no basis for assuming that students who learn to read through a steady diet of narrative texts will make an easy shift into reading across a variety of contexts. "Reading to learn" must be a part of reading experiences at all ages. Nonnarrative texts must be a part of the reading environment from the start. It is through frequent demonstrations with these kinds of texts that the developing reader learns to appreciate the multiple functions that reading serves in our lives and is also introduced to the flexible reading strategies that lead to success.

Setting aside these misconceptions we find a powerful place for the concept of flexibility in engaged reading. The appropriate conception of flexibility emphasizes the reader's skill at adjusting his or her reading strategies to the task demands—which includes consideration of the reader's goals, the text structure, and the social context. Creating a classroom environment where a variety of text types are available is the first step in building a context that nurtures flexibility—but only a first step. The second step is for these texts to be used in functional ways following demonstrations of engagement on the part of the teacher and class as a whole. Newspapers, magazines, and journals should be a part of the literary environment in the classroom. Teacher read-alouds should include not only stories but informational text as well. Book displays should include informational texts that help the students extend their inquiry beyond the four walls of the classroom. Technology and electronic texts should be a part of every classroom as well. Linda Labbo and her colleagues have demonstrated the many ways in which computer technology can be used effectively in early childhood settings to support literacy acquisition.

John Guthrie and his colleagues have demonstrated the importance of instruction in text search strategies as part of the CORI (Concept Oriented Reading Instruction) model.[10] One dimension of the CORI model—"Search and Retrieve"—is directed toward the skills and strategies associated with flexible reading. In the Search and Retrieve component the students are guided to learn how to search for subtopics related to their general interests and to search for informative sources. In one study, teachers modeled for students strategies for searching the index and table of contents to find specific information about such topics as life on the moon, craters, and space travel. Students were given an opportunity to apply these strategies in small cooperative group settings. Students successfully applied these strategies in a variety of complex learning tasks involving multiple text sources.

Teaching reading flexibility is also a major component in the transactional strategies model developed by Michael Pressley and his colleagues.[11] In one investigation of transactional strategies (using the SAIL—Students Achieving Independent Learning model), students were taught to adjust their reading to their specific purpose and to text characteristics (e.g., Is the material interesting? Does it relate to the reader's prior knowledge? What genre does the text fit? How difficult is the text?). The students were instructed to predict upcoming events (in narrative text) or information (in expository text), alter expectations as the text unfolds, generate questions and interpretations while reading, visualize represented ideas, summarize periodically, and attend selectively to the most important information. All of these processes were taught through direct explanations provided by teachers, teacher modeling, coaching, and studied practice, both in groups and independently. Here again, successful learning was achieved.

Flexibility in reading is taking on new dimensions as we move to increased use of an electronic medium for text. Through the work of David Reinking and Janet Watkins we have some indication of the potential for teaching flexibility through the use of HyperCard type programs.[12] They engaged elementary aged students in one of the most traditional kinds of academic tasks (i.e., writing a book report) only using a HyperCard program that involves multi-media presentations. Students were taught how to program in HyperCard up to the level of scripting. They learned how to use all of the HyperCard tools for drawing, copying, and pasting graphics, creating buttons and text fields, linking cards, and so forth. The lessons were specifically designed to prepare students to create multimedia book reviews.

Another interesting aspect of this research, in particular in terms of its relationship to flexibility, is the student being placed in the role of authoring text. In this way the student comes to understand the nature of the text structure. These understandings can then become internalized into flexible reading strategies. The book reviews (i.e., the data bases) were made available for use in central locations in the classrooms and school. Reinking and Watkins suggested that students were more engaged in learning and using the technology related to reading multimedia book reviews than in other academic activities in the classrooms.

Tests represent another interesting set of demands on flexibility. Although some might argue that tests (of the paper-and-pencil variety) represent an entirely unauthentic literacy task, the fact is that tests are an important reality in academic endeavors. Flexible strategies for test taking are crucial to performance that reveals underlying ability. Flexible strategies for test taking can and should be taught.

If fluency is the neglected goal in reading instruction, then flexibility must be regarded as the absent goal. There is both tremendous need and opportunity for us to offer effective instruction in this area.

## INDEPENDENT READERS SEEK MEANING

For the past several decades, we have, as a profession, struggled with the teaching of reading comprehension. We realized that attention to decoding alone was insufficient to prepare students to read beyond what they could say. Unfortunately, our focus on comprehension as a purely cognitive endeavor failed to tap into the depth of the reading experience. With the adoption of the engagement perspective, we have opened our perspective to include the cognitive, affective, and social dimensions of reading activity. Motivation, we now accept, must be considered as an integral part of the comprehension process. Why do people read? How are comprehension processes adapted to the reader's motivations? The three instructional principles that follow reflect current understandings of the compression process as a part of motivated literacy.

Readers seek meaning in text. It is not a meaning that lies dormant in the text that they must extract. It is a meaning that they must construct with the text. The concept of *Seeking* has a rich tradition in developmental psychology. Seeking out, exploring, and internalizing the surrounding world into explanatory mental models that must be constantly refined and expanded are central to most theories of intellectual, social, and moral development. The introduction to symbolic systems, language in particular, frees the learner from the limitations of physical interaction with the real world and enables higher level thinking to occur. Writing and reading enable the learner to engage at an even higher level.

In some cases, the meaning an individual seeks through reading is an experiential one. It is the reader motivated to enter and live within a virtual world created by an author. In this immersion in the text the reader may experience joy, pain, pleasure, distraction, escape, or any variety of emotional responses. In other cases, the meaning the reader seeks may have a more cognitive orientation. The reader is looking for information that can be used to build new knowledge structures or enhance old ones. In still other cases, the meaning the reader seeks may be of a critical nature. The reader is seeking insight and in doing so makes judgments and places value on the ideas in a text. Perhaps the reader is even formulating plans for action with the text. The motivations represented by these various purposes may be combined or may operate independently, but at the heart of each is the reader seeking meaning. In developing this perspective on reading as seeking, we draw heavily not only on the developmental theories of Piaget, Vygotsky, and Olson, but also on the work of Louise Rosenblatt and others in the area of reader response research. We divide our presentation of the seeking dimension of independent reading into three broad areas. We caution that these divisions are somewhat deceptive in the sense that readers seldom act in one mode or the other. Rather, these seeking processes tend to interact with one another during reading. They may ebb and flow during extended reading experiences, or perhaps even alter radically in a moment of reading.

## INDEPENDENT READERS SEEK EXPERIENCES THROUGH TEXT

**Instructional Principle 4: Effective reading instruction encourages students to engage aesthetically with text (see Fig. II.4).**

Louise Rosenblatt has proposed reader response as a useful analytical framework for understanding the reading comprehension process.[13] She argued that the act of reading must always be considered in terms of the reader's stance toward text. A particular stance reflects the motivations, purposes, and perspectives adopted by the reader. The stance a reader assumes toward a particular text exerts a strong influence on the processes and products of comprehension. Rosenblatt described one type or category of stance a reader may assume as aesthetic in nature. The reader lives in and through the text as he or she enters the meanings suggested by the author and constructed by his or her own imagination. A reader may become immersed in poetic language, evoking an emotional response that is much more affective than cognitive. A reader may enter a narrative and identity with a particular character. The reader is seeking the experience of the text itself. The goal is in the experience not in the details that are taken away from the text. Although we might think of this stance as associated with pleasure reading, the motivations and responses may go far beyond pleasure—indeed, the responses may go in opposite directions. What is essential to the aesthetic stance is the reader's motivation to immerse himself or herself in the text experience.

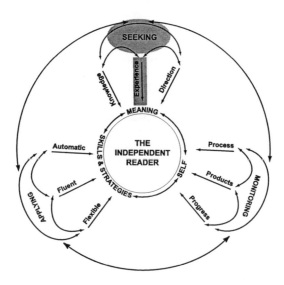

FIG. II.4.    The independent reader seeking experience.

The aesthetic stance is no trivial part of independent reading. A good portion of the independent, choice reading carried on by adults reflects this goal. And yet, what do we do in schools to encourage and prepare developing readers for this kind of text experience? The research data suggest that we do very little. Consider the following:

- The quality of the literature offered to students as part of beginning reading instruction, with traditional basals in particular, is poor. There is virtually no opportunity in these texts for the reader to engage aesthetically because these texts are devoid of multidimensional characters, rich forms of language expression, vivid imagery, complex plots, and/or powerful themes.
- The amount of time readers actually engage in connected reading in classrooms is severely limited. In the early primary grades, estimates of the average amount of connected reading time for an individual child are around 7 minutes per week.
- The typical instructional models employed by teachers to guide the reading of texts tends to force students away from aesthetic engagement with text and into a reading to remember mode of thinking.
- Readers are seldom given an opportunity to engage in free-choice reading for extended periods of time, from extended texts in a way that counts in the curriculum.

These assertions reflect the findings from classroom research as typical of elementary reading instruction. We emphasize that these characterizations do not represent or reflect the excellent teaching that goes on in many elementary classrooms. In fact, research in effective teachers' classrooms suggests specific strategies for engaging students in aesthetic reading experiences. These strategies include: building a quality storytime (read-aloud) program; engaging students in shared reading; organizing for small-group reading and discussion of texts; and establishing a personalized/individualized plan for independent reading.

## Storytime in the Classroom

Although most teachers describe reading aloud as a regularly occurring activity in their classrooms, it is typically regarded as more motivational than substantive, more peripheral than core, more expendable than critical, and more spontaneous than planful. Recent research into classroom read-aloud practices confirms that investments into a quality read-aloud program can pay off enormously in terms of reading development.

Roser and Hoffman conducted a series of studies focused on the building of a quality storytime experience for students.[14] They identified five elements of strong read-aloud programs. First, the read-aloud program must be given priority in the curriculum, and priority translates directly to time allotted. A quality program must be offered on a regular and recurring basis (a minimum of 25 minutes per day). Second, the program must introduce students to the best of children's literature. There is no substitute for good books that invite readers to enter the experience. Third, it is important that multiple texts be employed in a thematic structure that encourages students to explore the connections between authors, characters, themes, and topics. These combinations of texts may include picture books, chapter books, or combinations of the two. Fourth, personal response is encouraged, valued, and shared. Journal writing occurs in the context of a personal journal "quick write" after a storybook or a chapter has been read aloud. The invitation to write in their journals is offered in terms of: "Write whatever you are thinking or feeling about what we just read." Fifth, the sharing of responses and discussion (either in small groups or whole class settings) is crucial to a quality storytime experience. The teacher serves as catalyst for discussion through questioning, commenting, or sharing his or her own responses. And sixth, a public, visual/graphic record of thinking and response is important to solidify learning and connect the study of multiple texts. Roser and Hoffman recommended various strategies for collecting and organizing such public displays of response. These responses are recorded on a language chart (e.g., a large piece of butcher paper, a wall chart). In some cases the language charts are organized around the types of responses (e.g., observations, wonderings, connections—to life and literature) or on other occasions around the focus for a unit of study (e.g., Being Afraid: Who was afraid? What did they learn about being afraid?). Students are encouraged to add personal comments to the chart during the day as additional responses come to mind. The personal and private responses (in the journal), the public and shared responses (on the language chart), and the talk throughout the lesson encourage the development of critical thinking.

A quality storytime experience in the classroom offers students the opportunity to engage personally in extended narratives without regard for decoding ability. Students experience text and are motivated toward this purpose as they gain independence in their own reading skills and strategies.

## Shared Reading in the Primary Grades

The Shared Reading model, as described by Holdaway, is the "lap" method for teaching beginning reading brought into the classroom.[15] For many young children reading is first experienced in the home in the context of parents reading storybooks aloud to them. Favorite books are read again and again. Verbal interactions are accompanied by attention to the physical features of the books, the illustrations, and the text. Book talk between the parent and child focuses on the content but also on the ways in which many of the mechanical, technical, and conventional aspects of reading are experienced (e.g., book orientation, page turning, left-to-right/top-to-bottom text processing). Soon the child has memorized books and is mapping his or her stored knowledge of the text with the visual features of the print. For some children, this early mapping may lead to sight-word recognition and even the discovery of the alphabetic principle.

Holdaway's method, strikingly similar to the instructional principles articulated by Bill Martin in the mid-1960s through his *The Sounds of Language* series, provides teachers with a set of strategies for using physically enlarged text with highly predictable language patterns to scaffold the child from emergent to conventional forms of reading. Stories are read aloud with the teacher modeling fluent, expressive reading. The teacher focuses the students' attention on the print while the students follow along with the oral interpretation. The text is read repeatedly with the students. Each reading is accompanied by increased participation of the students in the reading. Students are encouraged to notice aspects of print and the reading process that will scaffold them toward greater independence.

The experience of reading in a shared reading model can be very much an aesthetic one, as described by Rosenblatt. "Aesthetic" is used here in the sense of the child becoming totally involved and immersed in the language of the story. The rhythms of the text and the participation with the text are motivating to the students. They, like the 3-year-old at home in his or her room selecting a book for a bedtime story, seek the experience of reading for the joy of it. Reading is a social experience in these contexts that sets the stage for a lifetime of choice reading.

## Book Clubs and Literature Circles

Students can develop sophisticated understandings of text through both teacher-led and peer-led discussion groups, learning to use a range of responses to address important themes and synthesize information. Raphael and McMahon coined the term, *Book Clubs* to refer to student-led discussions.[16] Their model consists of four components:

> *The reading* component focuses on daily reading of a literature selection. Different formats such as the teacher reading aloud, students reading silently, or students reading with a partner are used at different times.
>
> *The writing* component features students writing entries into logs such as critiquing, examining feelings, or sharing personal stories or responding to "think sheets" designed to elicit specific types of responses such as comparing and contrasting features of the book.
>
> *Community share* is the daily time for whole class discussions about the book or for the teacher to model discussion strategies.
>
> *Instruction* includes support in each of the areas.

Generally, students write an open-ended response to the text and bring it to the small, heterogeneously organized groups. Next, students engage in an open-ended discussion with others to express their personal feelings, make connections from their own lives to the literature, or clarify puzzling aspects of the text. Drawing or enacting scenes from the literature through drama can also provide opportunities to connect with the literature. In Betty Shockley's first-grade classroom, children reenacted stories to make personal connections, but also to learn how to sequence events and interact successfully in groups.[17]

Both the content of the literature students read (the "what") and the opportunities provided for students to discuss and share their interpretations of text (the "how") are important. Classrooms that are likely to facilitate lifelong, engaged, and critical readers combine the "what" with the "how" by providing opportunities to discuss high-quality literature.

Discussion and "book-talk" is only one, albeit highly important, avenue for response that encourages connections. Dramatizations, graphic/artistic responses to literature, media-based and technological responses, music, and movement are important to explore as well. We share Dorothy Strickland's view that any response activity that leads students to "live a little longer under the spell of a story" should be valued. Through diverse forms of response opportunities the multiple intelligences of students are tapped. A true interpretive community is formed in which students can observe and internalize multiple perspectives and critical stances toward literature experiences.

## Reader's Workshop

Promotion of independence in reading through personal models of instruction has a time-honored place in reading instruction. Jennette Veatch has written and spoken forcefully for over five decades on the merits of an Individualized Reading Approach.[18] Russell Stauffer was insightful in the ways in which he bridged a language experience approach to beginning reading instruction into a child-centered reading/writing curriculum.[19] Walter Barbee, in his writing on the Personalized Reading Approach, was articulate regarding the ways in which skill instruction (direct, explicit, and developmentally appropriate) could be included in a reading program that emphasized student choices.[20] Nancy Atwell has demonstrated the ways in which a readers workshop and a writers workshop that place a premium on choice and social interaction can be blended together within a functioning, manageable language arts program.[21]

The Reader's workshop emphasizes:

1. Free-choice reading by the students;
2. Time to read independently (or with others);
3. Talk (in the form of conferences over books that are being read) with the teachers and/or with peers;
4. Instruction (in the form of mini-lessons by the teacher) that address developing skills, strategies, and understandings; and,
5. Sharing of responses with others.

The reader's workshop model encourages students to behave in ways that are very much like the independent reading of mature adults. Whereas a good reader's workshop requires skill on the part of the teacher in terms of organizing, introducing, managing, and instructing, the students work quite independently. Even the most emergent readers can benefit from some time spent in a simplified reader's workshop environment (e.g., Drop Everything and Read [DEAR] time; Uninterrupted Sustained Silent Reading [USSR] time).

We caution that our description of these activities as useful in scaffolding students seeking experience with text, should not be interpreted to mean that these activity structures only involve the use of narrative or other literary genres of text. They can and should involve informational text and can and should involve students seeking understanding and seeking value. However, we do see these structures as contexts for students to have opportunities for aesthetic engagement. Taken together, these instructional activities (storytime, shared reading, book clubs, and reader's workshop) offer students the opportunity to engage in text experiences that promote aesthetic engagement. They differ as strategies in that they create a continuum of support for the students to develop independence as readers ranging from highly supportive (in storytime), to substantial support (in shared reading), to moderate support (in book clubs), to minimal support (in the reader's workshop). The teacher has a role in each of the models, although clearly the role becomes less direct moving along the continuum of support.

## INDEPENDENT READERS SEEK TO DEVELOP NEW KNOWLEDGE THROUGH TEXT

**Instructional Principle 5: Effective reading instruction encourages students to extend their conceptual knowledge base through text (see Fig. II.5).**

Clearly, narratives (stories) are important, familiar, and engaging for the young learner, and for this reason they have been relied on throughout the centuries in teaching children to read. But texts written to inform can excite the young reader as well. Children do wonder about their world, and texts can be a source of both satisfaction and stimulation for this curiosity. Texts written to inform can become the launching pad for inquiry. A curriculum that is designed to build on students' interests and questions must find a significant place for informational texts. Teachers must offer students experiences with texts that promote concept development, and teachers must be instructive about their use.

### Inquiry-Based Instruction as an Over-Arching Framework

Many educators have struggled with how to create an inquiry-based curriculum that can lead to the establishment of a more democratic society. An inquiry-based curriculum is based on the identification and solution of relevant

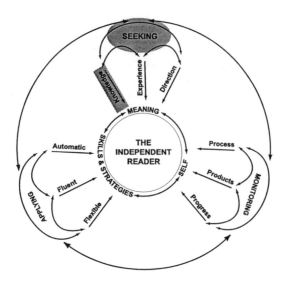

FIG. II.5.    The independent reader seeking knowledge.

problems from the concrete world. Students can gain information that is important to understanding the world through grappling with real-world problems. An engagement perspective has suggested that reading is a tool to foster growth in content knowledge and that integrating reading into content areas such as science and social studies throughout the day can facilitate children's higher level thinking.

Inquiry approaches have been used successfully at several different grade levels. Guthrie and his colleagues developed concept-oriented reading instruction (CORI). This approach involves students in observing and personalizing real-world problems, learning a variety of cognitive strategies for exploring problems, interacting socially, and communicating their understanding to genuine audiences. Fifth graders who were taught science and reading with this approach showed substantial growth in reading achievement. They also were more motivated than students in basal classrooms and gained in higher order cognitive strategies. Opportunities for observations, for developing concepts, and for interacting with others within the classrooms fostered students' achievement and motivation. Guthrie and his colleagues selected themes and designed a framework for units to be taught for 16 to 18 weeks each semester. The framework had four phases:

*Observe and personalize.* Students had opportunities to observe concrete objects and events in their natural world (e.g., observing trees, flowers, insects that seem interesting). Students then brainstormed and stated questions they wanted to explore with additional observations, data collection, and discussion. Students kept journals of their observations and personalized their interest by written questions. These were displayed throughout the classroom.

*Search and retrieve.* Students were encouraged to choose subtopics for more in-depth learning and to search for a variety of resources to answer their questions. Such resources as books, pictures, references, and videotapes offered explanations and information that led to other questions for exploration. Strategies for searching such as forming goals, categorizing, extracting, and synthesizing were taught explicitly through teacher modeling, guided practice, and teamwork.

*Comprehend and integrate.* Teachers taught students strategies for comprehending and integrating information using a variety of trade books, both informational texts and novels. Emphasis was on identifying topics, determining important details, and summarizing sections of the texts.

*Communicate to others.* Students became experts on the topics they researched and wanted to express their understanding to others. They developed synthesis projects to explain their findings to an audience. Students used a variety of forms such as reports, charts, class-authored books, dioramas, charts, and informational stories to communicate their findings.

An inquiry approach can also work quite successfully with younger children. Price and her colleagues studied Paula, a first-grade teacher who successfully adapted her reading instruction to reflect the advantages of integrated curriculum inquiry.[22] Paula's emphasis was on inquiry into topics of interest to her and her students (e.g., space, China, Brazil). The inquiry units encouraged student choice. For example, students had to decide on which area, such as flight, the solar system, or Jupiter they would explore in more depth when studying a space unit. Although the unit began as part of the science period, students incorporated their interest in space into other areas of the curriculum.

Paula spent a significant amount of time building students' background knowledge by introducing books and talking about them if children were not familiar with the topics. Students chose a topic to study in depth based on information. For example, after the teacher brought in both informational and narrative books about China, two students chose to research the Chinese New Year; several others made fortune cookies complete with fortunes written by the children after investigating Chinese food. Some students read Chinese fairy tales and rhymes, then wrote their own play using puppets that they presented at the Chinese Fair.

Students were involved in consulting different resources to answer the questions they had selected as research topics throughout the inquiry units. For example, students called a veterinarian when a question arose about whether dogs could get chicken pox after reading the book *Itchy Itchy*

*Chicken Pox*. Students had to learn the important reading strategy of using a telephone book to contact the veterinarian. Paula helped students focus on information-gathering strategies within the context of the inquiry units. Students learned to read for a purpose, learned how to skim for necessary information, and learned how to consult different kinds of resources (e.g., experts, telephone books, encyclopedias, or books). Paula used a variety of genres within the context of inquiry to encourage students to find out information and to utilize many important reading strategies.

Researchers and practitioners have worked together to identify successful inquiry-oriented practices and develop challenging, integrated curriculum. The examples illustrate how teachers involved students in inquiry-oriented curriculum that crossed traditional subject-area boundaries. Students read to solve concrete, real-world problems and teachers helped students to develop deep knowledge about important topics. When provided the opportunity to pursue topics of interest, even young children can learn research and communication strategies. Reading, then, serves as a tool for gaining information and concepts within real-world contexts.

## Vocabulary Development and Instruction

The seeking of new ideas and concepts is tied fundamentally to the process of vocabulary development. Vocabulary, considered both in terms of numbers of words recognized and the depth of understanding of word meanings, is the single best predictor of reading comprehension. Vocabulary development occurs not only as new words are learned; vocabulary development occurs as words move from one language system into another (e.g., from speaking vocabulary into writing vocabulary, from listening vocabulary into speaking vocabulary). Vocabulary development occurs as the meanings of known words are enriched and extended. The research literature on vocabulary is quite clear on several accounts. Three findings stand out, (a) almost any kind of systematic attention offered by the teacher to encourage vocabulary development in the classroom will produce positive learning results, (b) the focused study of a few words in depth tends to produce better results than superficial attention to large numbers of new words, and (c) words that are meaningful to the learner are those that will be learned most readily.

Following on these generalizations, we recommend that teachers systematically attend to vocabulary development as part of their reading instructional plan. We suggest that teachers target a small number of words each week (5–10) for the class to study. The selection of these words should be tied to the curriculum for that week. The new words should be introduced, taught, and assessed. The emphasis in the instruction should be on developing a depth of understanding of the underlying concept and the appropriate uses of the vocabulary in speaking and writing.

We also suggest that this direct instruction plan for vocabulary development be complemented with an individual vocabulary collection plan. Pauk has devised a plan for vocabulary development based on his concept of Frontier Words.[23] These are words that the student has some familiarity with (e.g., "I've heard that word a lot but I am not sure what it means") but no certainty as to their meaning. Each student is responsible for collecting frontier words on an ongoing basis. The words are recorded on cards and studied. The teacher is responsible for setting minimum expectations for the number of words collected (e.g., five new words per week), as well as a plan for assessment of the learning of the words.

These direct instruction and indirect instruction models for teaching vocabulary complement each other and promote concept development that is connected to the ongoing curriculum of study.

## Guided Reading Experiences That Promote Knowledge Acquisition

During the late 1960s, Russell Stauffer sternly criticized the prevailing model for teachers to guide students in the reading of text. The Directed Reading Activity (DRA) used in most basal reading programs of that time, was organized around Before Reading Activities (e.g., teaching new vocabulary, building conceptual background, motivating the reader), During Reading Activities (e.g., teacher purpose setting for silent reading, teacher questioning, oral re-reading), and After Reading Activities (e.g, discussion, extension, application, skills practice). Stauffer argued that this model was too teacher dominated and did not prepare the reader to do what would be expected and necessary in independent reading away from the teacher. He proposed an alternative structure that reflected more accurately what independent readers do as they read. In contrast to the DRA, his model could be internalized by the reader and applied successfully without the teacher during independent reading.[24]

Stauffer proposed the DRTA (Directed Reading Thinking Activity) as the alternative model. The DRTA framework involves a constant cycling of three phases, (a) predict, (b) read, and (c) prove. Independent readers are constantly making predictions about what is coming up in the text they are reading. They are engaging with the author's ideas, reflecting on the text, and evaluating its meaning for them. It is this process that teachers encourage in the DRTA model for guided reading. The teacher's role, according to Stauffer, should be one of intellectual agitator. The teacher encourages predictions, provides opportunities for extended reading, and challenges the readers to support their interpretations with reference to the text.

There have been numerous extensions and variations proposed over the years for guided reading. Most of these share in Stauffer's emphasis on the teacher as intellectual agitator. There are three areas of elaboration that are worth noting. The first has to do with the value of strategic and explicit talk on the part of the teacher during guided reading. Duffy and Roehler found in their research, for example, that explicit talk about the comprehension strategies good readers use when they read can yield enormous benefits to comprehension growth.[25] Explicit talk typically involves the teacher modeling the strategic thought processes he or she uses during reading and analyzing these process with the students. Sometimes the explicit descriptions are informal and heuristic in nature. At other times, the teacher may actually teach specific strategies for engaging with meaning in the text.

A second area of extension within guided reading has been in the area of social interaction. The research in this area suggests that group interaction (small group interaction in particular) is supportive of the development of comprehension processes. Small group interaction, with a skilled teacher's guidance, offers students an opportunity to experiment with comprehension strategies in a supportive context that is neither teacher dominated nor totally independent.

The third area of extension of guided reading has to do with individual differences. The range of differences in reading development within a given classroom can be enormous. Guided reading experiences provide students with an opportunity to interact with others who may be at similar or quite different points of development. The research in this area seems to suggest that flexible grouping on the part of the teacher can be enormously helpful in realizing the benefits of guided reading in nurturing independence. Here we find the teacher adapting the grouping patterns for students for guided practice with text. On some occasions the teacher may want homogeneity of ability or skills level (e.g., to refine or practice a particular strategy). In other instances the teacher may want a mixture of ability and skill levels so that a variety of strategies can be demonstrated and modeled.

The DRTA framework is designed for use with either narrative or expository text. Several strategies have been developed recently that are particularly adapted for the guided reading of expository materials where the goal is knowledge acquisition. Ogle has proposed a framework commonly referred to as KWL.[26] In using this strategy the teacher engages the students in a prereading conversation eliciting what the students already *Know* about the topic that is the focus for the reading and then what they *Want* to learn about the topic. All of the ideas suggested are recorded on a large, KWL chart. After the reading of the text, the teacher engages the students in a discussion about what they *Learned*. This information is added to the chart. The KWL framework has been expanded to include an extension where the students are encouraged to pursue the answers to questions they had before reading that were not addressed satisfactorily in the reading. Independent and small group research is encouraged.

Inquiry Charts and the I-Chart process offer another framework for teachers to support students in the acquisition of knowledge through reading.[27] Inquiry Charts emphasize the comparison of information gathered across a variety of texts sources. The Inquiry Chart process involves the following steps:

1. A topic for the inquiry is selected.
2. Key questions for the inquiry are identified.

3. Prior knowledge related to each question is shared and recorded.
4. Data sources (e.g., textbooks, journals, trade-books) are gathered and read.
5. Relevant information is recorded for the key questions.
6. Summary answers for each question are constructed.
7. Extended research is encouraged.
8. Reports are presented.

The I-Chart process can involve an entire class working together on an inquiry or it can be adapted for small cooperative learning groups, or it can be used as a framework to guide independent research.

Each of the instructional frameworks that have been described (i.e., DRTA, KWL, I-Charts, and Frontier Vocabulary collection) are designed as knowledge acquisition strategies that lend themselves to learning both inside and outside of formal school settings. They are designed to reflect the kinds of efficient and effective strategies that independent learners use regularly. The use of these frameworks strongly encourages and reinforces the development of flexible reading strategies.

## Fostering Critical Thinking and Critical Literacy

Knowledge is not just a neutral accumulation of facts and propositions. Knowledge involves beliefs and values. Teachers can encourage students to become critical in their analysis of texts, asking questions that explore author intent and assumptions. Simpson has summarized some strategies that encourage this kind of critical analysis:

- Setting questions (e.g., how else could the author have presented this material?)
- Disrupting the text (e.g., changing words, rewriting sections)
- Juxtaposing texts (e.g., comparing different accounts of the same event)
- Supplying alternative endings (e.g., writing a different outcome)
- Role playing, role reversal (e.g., uncovering what's been left out or what is inconsistent)
- Making insertions and additions (e.g., adding new information or someone else's view)
- Deleting (e.g., withholding or omitting information)
- Introducing parody (e.g., highlighting social and cultural assumptions and values through play)
- Examining the social context (e.g., Who wrote it, for whom, when, why?)[28]

We suggest that teachers be as bold in seeking out texts that challenge students to think and act critically as we are in seeking out texts that provide entertainment. We are not suggesting that the former replace the latter, but that we do offer both kinds of texts and purposes for our reading. The texts that invite a critical stance may be narrative or expository in nature. The common thread is that the texts invite us to examine our values and spur us to take action on issues that we should address as individuals living in and contributing to a democratic society. There are any number of points from which to launch such investigations that involve critical literacy. The "big idea" issues (e.g., the environment, health and health care, religious freedom, sexism, democracy) are all around us.

We suggest that teachers be bold in reaching outside the traditional four walls of the classroom and the school building into the community where literacy events are played out daily. Unless we demonstrate how literacy influences their lives and how they can control literacy to shape the events in their lives, we will have succeeded in situating literacy solely as a school exercise. Building these home–school–community connections is not easy, but the potential for gain justifies the effort.

Currently, theorists and researchers are developing new models to conceptualize teaching and learning that more closely reflect students' home backgrounds and view student diversity as an asset to building a more democratic society. Conceptions of literacy that are socially based suggest that children learn culturally appropriate ways of using language and constructing meaning from texts in their early years at home. Virtually all children in a literate society have numerous experiences with print before coming to school because literacy practices are embedded within the social fabric of family life. Young children learn the meaning of print by being surrounded by it in their immediate environment, through their explorations in play, and understanding its role in their everyday lives.

Yet, different cultural groups have unique and complex ways of integrating written language with daily social life. For example, students have different ways of interpreting texts, telling stories, asking questions, or providing explanations. Some of these ways more closely match school-based practices than others, sometimes resulting in miscommunication between teacher and student.

Some of the major barriers to student success have been the deficit view of students from diverse backgrounds, the focus on skills and drills, and the mismatch between home and school practices. The deficit view sees minority homes as providing limited language-learning environments and placing little value on education. This view has led to continued drill and practice on basic decoding skills for nonmainstream students whereas the White, middle-class students receive instruction more focused on reading for meaning.

Studies that have focused on the school context have also identified successful strategies for linking home and school. Several studies have illustrated successful discourse strategies that match students' backgrounds; others have identified school practices that build on community practices; and others have identified successful teachers of particular communities. Au found that teachers who had been successful with native Hawaiian students developed talk-story-like reading lessons to better match students' out-of-school discourse styles.[29] In a similar way Puerto Rican teachers allowed students to take the floor without having to be called on—a style consistent with everyday conversation.

Researchers such as Ada found that students were quite successful when teachers used community practices as the basis for informing school practices.[30] Such practices as encouraging students to write about family interactions and life histories of community members were among the most popular with students. In collaboration with teachers, Moll and Gonzalez established the "funds of knowledge" project to identify community resources and use them in classrooms.[31] Teachers document the activities of households and the social networks that facilitate economic assistance and labor cooperation. Ladson-Billings identified teachers who were successful with African-American students and defined a "culturally based pedagogy" that includes considering students as competent learners while extending their thinking. These studies have in common understanding and valuing students as individuals within cultural contexts.[32]

Teachers face enormous challenges in learning to understand the cultural contexts in which their students live. However, a first step toward linking home and school experiences is for teachers to value the knowledge that students bring from home and see it as the basis from which teachers can build. The teacher can then build on existing knowledge through dialogue. Being informed about individual students and understanding students' larger social cultural backgrounds lays a foundation for making more explicit connections between home and school. While teachers can send books and other materials home from school to help students with needed strategies to succeed in school, teachers can also value students' identities and backgrounds and bring their experiences into the school to facilitate stronger home–school–community connections.

## INDEPENDENT READERS SEEK GUIDANCE AND DIRECTION THROUGH TEXT EXPERIENCES

**Instructional Principle 6: Effective reading instruction supports students as they engage with texts that provide guidance and direction (see Fig. II.6).**

"How to" texts are ubiquitous. They are not just a part of cookbooks and travel guides; they are present in a variety of forms and formats ranging from signs, to charts, to hyper-texts. Most of our research into reading comprehension has tended to ignore interaction with these kinds of texts and these purposes in favor of an examination of the process of literary response (Principle #4) or learning from text, where the goal is more specifically tied to the formation of concepts, beliefs, and attitudes (Principle #5). Perhaps it is in their commonplace nature that this purpose and these texts tend to be ignored. Perhaps it is

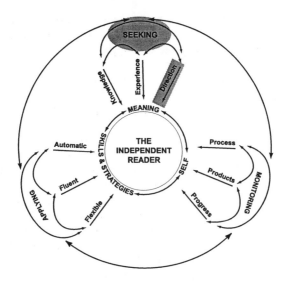

FIG. II.6.   The independent reader seeking direction.

in the diverse nature of the physical appearance and design of these texts (e.g, signs, pamphlets, charts) that they tend to be ignored. Perhaps it is for the lack of a good theoretical basis for looking at these texts that they tend to be ignored. And yet, engaging with text for guidance and direction may be the most common form of reading for most people, most often. Tom Sticht, in a study of adult readers, found that 75% of the reading done on the job was what he called "reading to do".[33] We know surprisingly little from our research regarding the features of good text design to support this kind of reading. Nor do we have a great deal of information of the nature of the strategies that are most effective in supporting processing. Clearly, readers who seek this kind of meaning will employ flexible reading strategies (Principle #3) given that the range of texts that are coincidental with this purpose tend to be diverse. In discussing this principle, we focus on some of the problems associated with the reading of procedural texts and then discuss some of the practical issues related to instruction.

## The Problem(s) With Reading Procedural Texts

One problem that can be encountered in considering procedural texts is that these texts are often ignored. For example, surveys and interviews have revealed that over 30% of individuals buying consumer products would not read the directions. They may believe that reading and understanding the instructions may be more difficult than the alternatives available (e.g., guessing, following a model).

A second problem with procedural texts is that even when they are read, they are often not well understood. Kammann estimated that even when instructions are read, for example, they are understood only about two thirds of the time.[34] Whether this failure is the result of the text being poorly organized or presented, or the result of a reader who is apprehensive and struggling with an activity in a need to know state of mind and not reading carefully, or a reflection of a reader who has limited basic text-processing skills and limited strategies for reading this kind of text, we can only speculate. It is quite likely that all of these factors, and others, contribute to the situation.

A third problem with the reading of procedural texts is that we are seldom taught how to use them effectively. Most reading methods texts ignore the topic totally. Most basal reading programs fail to offer experiences with these kinds of text in their programs, and even when they do they fall short on the explicit teaching of instruction in strategies for effective use. If instruction and experiences are offered at all, they tend to appear late in the middle-school years or secondary reading curriculum.

A fourth problem is that procedural texts often make assumptions about the reader's understanding of symbol systems that are used with little explanation or support. They may be cryptic—not just in the sense of being short but also in the sense of using codes that are unfamiliar. A simple example of this would be road signs, in particular road signs that use the international symbol system (i.e., the wordless road signs). More complex examples involve the use of icons that may not be familiar (e.g., the scripted "i" sign for information).

A fifth problem has to do with the increasing complexity of text structures that require strategic control over complex processing patterns. Electronic texts provide the best example of this increasingly complex structure for texts. Hyper-text includes complex levels of text imbedded within texts. There are no uniform patterns for these text structures. Each is unique. Typically these texts, which may be ultimately directed toward providing new knowledge, are accompanied by procedural text features that must guide the reader into the text as a resource. As these texts become more commonplace in our literacy context, we will need to bring better skills to the use of these kinds of mixed texts.

The solution to these problems rests, in part, in good instruction. This instruction must begin at the earliest levels of educational programming and does not wait until the student has control over the basic skills. These are basic skills of reading.

## TEACHING WITH PROCEDURAL TEXTS
## AND FOR PROCEDURAL PURPOSES

We have compiled a list of suggestions regarding the use of procedural texts in classrooms. These represent a combination of activities, strategies, and content-tied lessons that can be combined and adapted across grades and developmental levels.

1.   Fill your classroom with procedural texts. This includes both informal and published works. Be sure that the kinds of texts that you provide are functional and support the students in achieving their learning goals. Examine your classroom for procedural/organizational routines that require some interaction with your students. Are there ways to achieve these same purposes with a text system or plan? For example, checking role is a typical classroom routine. Can this be guided by a set of text directions and response opportunities? Lunch money, absence reports, and so forth can all be proceduralized in terms of some guiding text directions.

Classroom rules, procedures, and consequences can also be specified in terms of procedural texts and signs. Classwork assignments can be laid out for the students in work contracts that are designed for the class, groups, or individual students. Research/inquiry guides can become quite sophisticated as procedural texts for students to follow in independent research. Include class schedules for the students in a public place as well as on personal systems.

2.   Read the room, your school, and your community for procedural texts. This activity grows out of Frierre's notion of reading the word/reading the world for the ways in which texts are used to define relationships, access, and control.[35] One way to approach such an activity is to adapt Halliday's framework for the functions of language to an examination of the texts that the student encounters.[36] Halliday studied children's use of oral language and discovered seven functions evident in the talk of young children:

1. Instrumental: Children use language to satisfy personal needs and to get things done.
2. Regulatory: Children use language to control the behavior of others.
3. Personal: Children use language to tell about themselves.
4. Interactional: Children use language to get along with others.
5. Heuristic: Children use language to find out about things, to learn things.
6. Imaginative: Children use language to pretend, to make believe.
7. Informative: Children use language to communicate something for the information of others.

Such a system can be simplified for students (individually, with partners, in groups, or as a class) to examine the texts that are around them and the functions they reflect. Extending this to specific topic of procedural texts it would be identifying those texts that describe how to. Extending it into a Frierrian model would involve having the students examine control and relational issues (who wrote the text, for what purpose, to what audience). This is not a task for older students. Kindergarten and primary-grade children can find this kind of exercise enlightening.

3.    Try to make the procedural texts you offer interactive. Procedural texts that require interaction and engagement are more likely to be attended to in the context of instruction. Interactive texts can be as simple as checking off steps as they are completed or requiring more sophisticated responses. Interactive texts require that the reader attend to the detail and, if appropriate, the linear processing and use of the text.

4.    Teach the use of procedural texts. Be explicit about how the procedural texts in the environment are to be used. Model the process of use. Conduct guided practice with the text. Reinforce appropriate use of the text. Hold students accountable.

5.    Write these texts with students. Procedural texts that are composed with the students are likely to lead to understanding at a deeper level. This kind of coconstruction of texts can begin simply with the signs in a classroom, but can be extended to more elaborate forms of text. Huntley-Johnston, Merritt and Huffman offered some excellent guidelines and strategies for writing how-to books with high school students.[37] These strategies can be adapted for use with younger children as well.

6.    Emphasize texts that rely on symbols/graphics as much as they rely on common words and sentence structures. Introduce students to international symbols for regulatory signs, and so forth as a way of reinforcing the concept of texts without words.

7.    Create texts that support problem-solving strategies. What do you do when you can't recognize a word you are reading? What do you do when you don't understand a word meaning? What do you when you are unsure of an author's meaning? These are problem solving situations, common to literacy acts, that we will discuss extensively in the next principle of proficient reading. Our point here is that procedural texts can be represented for students in terms of explicit strategies.

8.    Games are a motivating context for teaching about procedural texts. Rules for games can become quite complicated in their structure. They present an opportunity for a close reading and interpretation of texts.

9.    Computers and computer programs also offer an excellent opportunity for using and adapting procedural texts. Directions for the use of the computer itself or specific software programs are a starting place. More complex would be the actual writing of simple computer programs that require the creation of how to texts for computers to read and follow. Computers and programming offer us a wonderful opportunity for modeling thinking processes in quite explicit ways.

10.    Consider all of the specific opportunities associated with content area teaching. Science experiments lend themselves to procedural texts, guides, and manuals. Research strategies in the content areas can be framed in terms of specific steps to follow in the inquiry process with supporting text guides and

graphic organizers. Theater and drama provide an opportunity to deal with procedural texts (e.g., stage directions) embedded in a text that has a different function. Language arts instruction using a workshop model can include book publishing, editing procedures, and so forth and related procedural texts to support successful outcomes.

We offer these as starting points to begin the conversation in your classroom regarding procedural texts and their uses. These forms of engagement will lead to the development of appropriate skills and strategies.

## INDEPENDENT READERS SELF-MONITOR

The development of independence in reading ultimately involves taking control over the reading process. Independence does not mark the end of development. Independence in reading becomes the framework for the individual to expand his or her literacy over a life-time. Clay describes one aspect of this control in terms of the developing reader becoming self-extending. The reader self-monitors the processes of sense-making during the act of reading and is able to adapt strategies to resolve blockages to meaning. Strategy selection and strategy application are a fundamental part of this self-monitoring and control process. But control from an engagement perspective has an even broader sense. Control for the independent reader also involves an awareness of reading as it fits into the individual's values, choices, and perspectives.

## INDEPENDENT READERS SELF-MONITOR THE PROCESS OF READING

**Instructional Principle 7: Effective reading instruction encourages students to self-monitor as they read so they can adjust their reading strategies as necessary (see Fig. II.7).**

When task demands are relatively easy, the independent reader appears effortless and fluid in the act of reading. Increase the task demands far enough, however, and even the most skilled reader will show signs of hesitation and even frustration. For the early reader, not so far along the developmental path, the struggle with demanding text is more a way of life than an exception. This is as it should be. Only through venturing into the more challenging kinds of text experiences will the developing reader grow in underlying abilities. Some of the challenges may require support external to the reader such as the guidance of a teacher. So called *teachable* moments arise as the learner engages in tasks at this level. Some challenges, however, may be addressed successfully by the reader through reflection and strategic responses. These are opportunities for learners to apply their self-extending systems that lead toward independence.

Peeking into the reflective aspects of the reading process is no easy matter. Perhaps the most revealing looks into the reading process have come through the qualitative examination of reading errors (miscues). Goodman and his colleagues have developed fairly sophisticated strategies for interpreting student performance in relation to reader reliance on surrounding cue sources. The

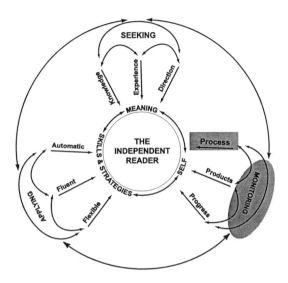

FIG. II.7.   The independent reader self-monitoring the processes of reading.

analysis of self-correction strategies has been particularly valuable in that it suggests readers actively monitor their sense making. Proficient readers tend to ignore miscues that do not affect meaning, but will typically engage in self-corrections of miscues that violate the syntactic or semantic constraints of the material being read. Readers exhibit a wide variety of fix-up strategies ranging from simple rereading of text leading up to the miscue up to a phonetic analysis of the unknown word.

Peeking into the comprehension processes in a similar on-line fashion has proven to be even more challenging. Some researchers have embedded text incongruities and then looked for evidence that the reader has noticed the inconsistency and what the reader did to resolve the meaning blockage. In other cases, researchers have asked readers to "think-aloud" as they read with the goal of inspecting patterns of connection and reflection during the process. For the most part, studies of these types suggest that the reader is remarkably focused on making sense of the text and will often ignore irrelevant or inconsistent information in staying with the coherent representation of meaning. Readers who are struggling with the text in decoding and comprehension tend to be more erratic in their response patterns. Self-correction patterns, for example, are less consistent in terms of which errors are addressed. Meaning-blockages in comprehension tend to be ignored rather than dealt with in a strategic way.

Many researchers have tried to nurture independence and reflection through both direct and indirect methods. For example, Paris, Cross, and Lipson taught third and fifth graders explicit strategies prompted by metaphors such as "Be a reading detective" and followed up by providing feedback and opportunities to apply the strategies in different contexts.[38] Duffy, Roehler, and their colleagues guided teachers in ways to give detailed explanations of strategies. Students displayed increased awareness of strategies after exposure to these direct methods.[39]

As theories about the role of social context have gained in importance, researchers have developed instructional methods that involve peers in the identification and sharing of strategies. For example, Palincsar and Brown developed reciprocal teaching in which students were taught to use predicting, questioning, clarifying, and summarizing, and then in they turn taught these to their peers.[40] Peer support was also used in Stevens and his colleagues" cooperative grouping model.[41] Modeling, peer tutoring, and cooperative activities were features that provided opportunities for students to discuss content and processes of reading. These studies suggest that specific methods can enhance students" ability to monitor their processes and that the social context plays a major role in supporting students" understanding of strategies.

Langer and Applebee suggested five important components of instruction that support the development of metacognitive strategies: ownership, appropriateness, structure, collaboration, and transfer of control.[42] Students need to develop a sense of ownership over what they read and write. Instruction needs to be designed that is appropriate to the developmental level of the learner, whereas the structure of the task needs to fit students' needs. Promoting collaboration among peers is essential for students to share the strategies they are learning with each other. The ultimate goal of instruction is to transfer control to students; they need to be responsible for regulating their own learning.

An important aspect of instruction that aids students in developing metacognitive strategies is dialogue. Children's ability to talk about language is an indicator of their metacognitive processes. Thus, students need many opportunities to talk about their ideas and strategies. Galda, Shockley, and Pellegrini found multiple opportunities for students to talk with one another in Betty Shockley's classroom.[43] The more students talked with each other in diverse groups, the more they used language that was positively related to literacy development. Shockley's first-grade classroom was characterized by the following opportunities for students to interact:

> *Oral Sharing* time not only allowed students to talk about their home experiences, but provided a forum for students to retell familiar stories, rehearse stories they would later write about, and increase awareness of the language they were using.

> *Writing Workshop* allowed students to become aware of various cognitive strategies as students helped each other sound out words, spell, and com-

pose stories. Discussing students' stories promoted attention to detail, awareness of the role of the audience, and helped children internalize the writing strategies of others.

*Reading Workshop* in which students read self-selected books allowed students to become aware of and practice reading strategies with other students. Students often helped each other decode words, shared aspects of the story, or alternated reading aloud pages with a partner. *Whole Class Reading* focused on the teacher reading a Big Book or other book aloud. Students not only talked about events and characters, but also about strategies for understanding print. The dramatic reenactments that often followed the story provided students with opportunities to transform their understanding of the story and to use dialogue in meaningful ways.

*Project Centers* provided another means using oral language in meaningful ways to monitor their own understanding of texts. Students chose to do dramatic readings, plays, or other relevant activities that provided opportunities to think aloud through talk.

All of these features of the classroom allowed students opportunities to learn from one another and to become aware of the purposes and processes of making sense of print. Within each of the activity areas, students were using oral language to enhance their own understandings of print and to become increasingly able to regulate their own learning.

In a second-grade classroom studied by Commeyras and Sumner, dialogue was again a central feature of classroom interaction.[44] In this classroom the focus was on students' questions about literature. Students were quite willing to generate many questions when given the opportunity and expressed a desire to communicate what perplexed them to others. However, privileging certain kinds of questions or assuming a hierarchy to questions (such as Bloom's) tended to stifle students' questions. Their study suggests that teachers need to establish supportive contexts in which students can pose questions that are important to them about texts. Questions are another form of talk that allows students to monitor their own understanding of the material.

As theory and research have moved to embrace a social model of learning, it is clear that classroom talk will play an increasingly important role in the development of self-monitoring strategies. No longer are researchers and teachers suggesting that reading is a process that occurs within an individual's head; instead, decoding, comprehending, and monitoring of one's own processes are enhanced through social interaction. The teacher and peers are central to helping students make the internal reading processes external, and thus, allowing students' increased control over processes. However, there is an important caution when considering teacher and student dialogue—just any classroom talk will not necessarily facilitate students' self-monitoring. Talk must be focused on the task, appropriate to students' developmental levels, and facilitative rather than restrictive. When students' ways of talking do not match the teacher's because of differences in cultural backgrounds, miscommunication and alienation can occur. It is essential for teachers to be sensitive to students' backgrounds and thoughtful about participation structures that will enhance opportunities for all students to engage in meaningful literacy activities.

## INDEPENDENT READERS SELF-MONITOR THE PRODUCTS OF THEIR READING

**Instructional Principle 8: Effective reading instruction encourages students to self-monitor the products of their reading experiences.**

The distinction offered here between Principle 7, focused on process, and Principle 8, focused on products, is subtle but important. Instructional Principle 7 deals with on-line self-monitoring. The reader is self-monitoring performance and making strategic adjustments in relation to purpose and task demands. Instructional Principle 8 is focused on the reader's reflecting on the products of reading. Here we find readers asked to examine, analyze, and interpret some products of reading (typically their own, but perhaps those of others).

Yetta Goodman and her colleagues have pioneered the use of a strategy termed *retrospective miscue analysis* that encourages the reader to engage in this kind of self-reflection on reading products.[45] The techniques for retrospec-

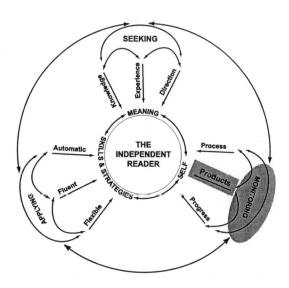

FIG. II.8.    The independent reader self-monitoring the products of reading.

tive miscue analysis are evolving in both research and in instructional applications. There are essentially four steps involved in retrospective miscue analysis:

1. Initial session with the reader.
2. Preparation for the RMA session.
3. Conducting the RMA session.
4. Follow-up of the RMA session.

During the first step, the teacher engages the reader in a traditional reading miscue inventory activity. The reader is asked to read aloud from challenging text without the assistance of the teacher. Later, the reader is guided in a retelling or summary statement of the story that has been read. The session is tape recorded. In preparing for the RMA session, the teacher has the option of providing the student with an unmarked or marked (i.e., with the miscues indicated) copy of the text to follow along. If the teacher chooses to preselect the miscues for analysis then he or she should focus on a limited number of miscues (say five to ten and one or two strategies (e.g., self-correction). During the RMA session, the teacher sits with a student as he or she listens to a replaying of the reading performance. If an unmarked text is used, the reader is in control of the tape recorder. The reader stops the tape whenever he or she notices a discrepancy between the text and the oral reading. The reader talks about the processes he or she was or was not using at that point in time. The reader may suggest strategies he or she should have used but didn't. The teacher's questions focus on strategies such as: "Does the miscue make sense?" "Does the miscue look like what was on the page?" "Why do you think you made the miscue?" If the teacher is using preselected miscues, then the teacher controls the tape recorder. The discussion is similar in terms of the reader's responsibility for explaining strategies, but the teacher may be more direct in pointing out the similarities across the miscues based on the patterns he or she has selected. The follow-up sessions may involve direct instruction in new strategies that can be helpful to the reader. Follow-up sessions may involve repeated experiences with RMA under more focused conditions (e.g., particular types of miscues, and/or particular straggles).

The goal for RMA is that the reader will eventually internalize these reflective strategies and incorporate the lessons learned into productive strategies that can be applied on-line during reading.

Another area that has received considerable attention is in rubric development and application. Instruction that involves reflection on products using rubrics has entered the language arts through the area of writing. As holistic assessment of writing has grown in popularity, in particular in state-wide, high-stakes assessments, we have seen an increased use of rubrics to grade, score, or otherwise place value on particular writing products. It is not at all unusual in states where holistic assessments of writing performance are mandated to see teachers structuring lessons around the application of rubrics for quality writing. In some cases, these rubrics are applied to writing products brought in from external sources. In others, students are expected to apply these rubrics to their own writing products.

This basic strategy is being applied to reading tasks that require the students to generate some sort of product that demonstrates text comprehension or interpretation. For example, students in a class may be expected to write brief book reviews as part of an independent reading or home reading program. A rubric is developed that describes the important elements, features, or qualities of a book review. These qualities may be described in terms of scale ranging from substandard to excellent. The rubric may be imported from some external source, or it may be developed collaboratively by the class with teacher guidance. In the case of local development of norms, the teacher guides the students in an analysis of a mixture of reviews of the same book. What are the qualities that make one review better than another? Can we describe these qualities in terms that can be applied across a wide range of responses? The students are engaged in practice sessions in which they "score" reviews and come to some general agreement on the norms for excellence. Later, the students may be asked to self-evaluate some of their own reviews. This kind of self-assessment of reading products is designed to feed-forward into the students own comprehension processes and work on products. As students internalize the norms for good products, they adapt their on-line comprehension strategies to be more productive.

## INDEPENDENT READERS SELF-MONITOR THEIR PROGRESS AND DEVELOPMENT

**Instructional Principle 9: Effective reading instruction encourages the reader to self-monitor his/her development and progress in literacy, and to use this knowledge to set short and long-term personal learning goals.**

All human activity is goal directed—which is not to say that all human activity is necessarily rational. Some goal-directed activity is innate (e.g., breathing). Some goal-directed activity is dysfunctional (e.g., drug abuse). In the case of literacy, however, there is a more socialized and rational base for goal-directed activity. Literacy is both a means and an end. Individuals seek entertainment or information through reading. Individuals also seek to improve their reading ability as a means of gaining greater access to entertainment and information. Most current theories of motivation suggest that individuals will put effort into reaching goals that they perceive as achievable and desirable. If we can provide developing readers with a record of where they have been, with details on where they are, with some sense of the steps on the path that are ahead, and with some assurance that they can achieve these steps given reasonable amounts of effort, we can enhance motivation.

Current theories of the motivation process suggest that the following factors exert a strong positive influence on activity:

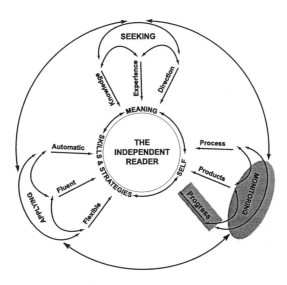

FIG. II.9.    The independent reader self-monitoring his or her progress in reading.

- The value an individual places on a task or goal determines whether or not the individual will expend the effort necessary to accomplish it.
- Goals are most likely to be pursued if they are personally relevant and important.
- Individuals are more willing to engage in activities, even those that are not of inherent interest, if the ultimate goal is of personal value.
- Students who perceive a task as important will engage in the task in a more planful and effortful manner.
- An individual's sense of personal competence at achieving a goal directly influences that person's decision to pursue the goal.
- A cooperative learning environment is more likely to support students' motivation toward a goal than a competitive environment.
- The teacher can enhance motivation by encouraging the students to adopt a learning-oriented (How can I do this task? What will I learn?), rather than a performance-oriented stance (How will I look? What will others think about me?).
- Goal specificity, challenge, and proximity are important determinants of engagement in achievement tasks.

In what ways can and should these understandings regarding motivation inform our plans for instruction? One clear point of contact between these findings and practice comes through a consideration of plans for assessment.

An effective reading program can encourage self-monitoring on the part of the developing reader by offering a plan for assessment that is grounded in a developmental perspective of literacy acquisition and designed to yield performance data useful in documenting progress toward learning goals. Traditionally, assessment plans for reading have tended to rely exclusively on norm-referenced, standardized tests that are informative neither to teachers nor to students. Assessment schemes that rely exclusively on criterion-referenced tests suffer from the same limitations. It is only through the development and application of authentic and ongoing performance assessment plans that teachers and students are informed in a meaningful way. Through the use of portfolios and other features of alternative assessment plans, the student becomes a part of the learning process. Short-term and long-term goals are negotiated, and motivation is fostered.

Research into the use of portfolios as the basis for a comprehensive assessment plan in the reading/language arts areas has demonstrated its superiority over traditional models. Through the adoption of portfolios, students and teachers share in the responsibility for not only documenting growth in skill, but also in the process of setting short-term and long-term goals. Portfolios require that students reflect on themselves as learners and engage in planning for focusing future effort. Afflerbach explained that portfolios can document complex and interrelated aspects of students' growth and achievement. Furthermore, he found that a portfolio can accommodate an expanded range of reading outcomes and time frames associated with an engagement perspective on reading.

Portfolios serve a number of purposes, depending on the needs of the classroom or school in which they are used:

- Portfolios can serve as repositories for the history of students' development and accomplishment in engaged reading tasks and outcomes,
- Portfolios can be used to demonstrate the range of students' accomplishments related to complex tasks of engaged reading to parents, administrators, teachers, and students themselves,
- Portfolios can help students develop reflective and critical perspectives on their own work across the school year, familiarize students with the ways and means of assessment, and contribute to student independence in assessing their own performance.

Although there has been ample documentation of the positive contribution of portfolio assessment strategies on students' motivations and growth, concerns have been raised over the practical issues involved in the use of such plans. Stakeholders in education who are outside the immediate classroom context for learning may regard the assessment aspects of portfolios with suspicion. These data may be regarded as highly subjective and not very useful in making comparisons of individual student performance to commonly recognized standards for achievement. On what basis should policy makers and program leaders make their decisions when the objective data from standardized testing are not available? Some research suggests that the feasibility of maintaining two parallel systems of assessment (i.e., the internal one for teachers and students and parents that is portfolio based; and the external one for administrators, policy makers, and the public that is test based) is impossible in the real world. At the philosophical level the two systems are at loggerheads with the latter showing total disregard for the motivational aspects of reading development. At the practical level, the demands of maintaining two systems—with one not valued outside the classroom and the other not valued within the classroom—can prove overwhelming.

Valencia and Au have studied the use of portfolios in different contexts with both research sites addressing such issues as: how well portfolios document literacy learning that is both authentic and aligned with curriculum; teachers' ability to interpret and evaluate portfolio evidence from more than one site; and what teachers learn about literacy instruction and assessment as a result of cross-site collection.[46] They found that as teachers closely examine students' work, they clarify important learning outcomes and learn to interpret student performance on multiple forms of evidence. They found teachers capable of high levels of agreement in evaluating students (across research sites) based on portfolio evidence. Agreement levels were influenced by the presence of a strong rubric for evaluation.

Hoffman and Worthy reported work with a group of teachers in a major metropolitan school district who had joined together to do away with standardized testing at the first-grade level.[47] Working collaboratively, school-based and university-based educators designed an alternative assessment plan. The PALM (Primary Assessment of Language Arts and Mathematics) model focuses on three strategies for data collection:

> On-going (curriculum-embedded) assessments that involve the careful inspection, interpretation, and documentation of students engaged in classroom tasks,

> Taking-a-closer-look assessments that involve the selective use of informal assessments for particular purposes and for particular students,

> Demand assessments that involve the administration of standardized tasks across a number of classrooms and the interpretation of performance of individual students in relation to the participating group.

The data collected through these strategies become part of a portfolio that contains not only work samples but also a developmental checklist documenting student progress over time. The results of an evaluation study of this model indicate that a carefully designed performance assessment plan with a portfolio base can provide data useful to both internal and external audiences. The PALM model yields data that is useful to teachers and students to encourage reflection and goal setting. It also yields data that can be used on a normative basis to compare a student or group of students' academic progress to a referent group. Based on the results of this study, the school district has moved to implement the PALM model as a substitute for standardized testing. Furthermore, the district is now piloting the use of the model throughout the primary grades.

Retrospective interviews with teachers implementing the model suggest several cautions. First, implementation of portfolio system requires considerable staff development and a supportive climate. Second, implementation and maintenance of a portfolio system requires considerable effort beyond that typically associated with traditional forms of assessment. The motivation for the teacher must be more than just to derive a score on a student at the end of the year. The motivation must be tied to better ongoing instructional decision making on the part of the teacher, and enhanced reflection on the part of learners regarding their progress toward their literacy goals.

## SUMMARY

These nine principles, derived from research, suggest some important understandings for how reading instruction can make a difference in the development of balanced reading. Furthermore, the principles suggest specific actions, in terms of tools, activity structures, and teaching strategies that can be used to promote growth. And finally, these principles suggest the beginning of a decision-making basis from which teachers can continue to grow and learn independently.

To what degree are these instructional principles already in place in elementary classrooms around the country? To what degree do these principles reflect an idealized world that is outside the realm of possibility for most classroom teachers? These are questions we explore in depth in Part III of this book.

## NOTES

1. Price, D., & Hoffman, J. V. (1998/1999). Teaching students to decode in first grade: Back to the old phonics, or on to the new? *The State of Reading, 5*(1), 39–48.
2. Gaskins, I. W. (1996/1997) Procedures for word learning: Making discoveries about words. *Reading Teacher, 50*(4), 312–327.
3. Cunningham, P., & Cunningham, J. W. (1992). Making words: Enhancing the invented spelling–decoding connection. *Reading Teacher, 46*(2), 106–115.
4. Allington, R. L. (1980). Fluency: The neglected reading goal in reading instruction. *Reading Teacher, 36*, 556–561.
5. Stahl, S. A., Heubach, K. L., & Crammond, B. (1997). *Fluency-oriented reading instruction* (Reading Research Report No. 79). Athens, GA: Universities of Georgia and Maryland, National Reading Research Center.
6. Blum, I. H., Koskinen, P. S., Tennant, N., Parker, E. M., Straub, J., & Curry, C. (1995). Using audiotaped books to extend classroom literacy instruction into the home of second language learners. *Journal of Reading Behaviour, 27*(4), 535–563.

7.  Guszak, F.J. (1992). *Reading for students with special needs*. Dubuque, IA: Kendall/Hunt.
8.  Fountas, I. C., & Pinnell, G. S. (1996). *Guided reading: Good first teaching for all children*. Portsmouth, NH: Heinemann.
9.  Carver, R. P. (1990). *Reading rate: A review of research and theory*. San Diego, CA: Academic Press.
10. Guthrie, J. T., Van Meter, P., McCann, A. D., Wigfield, A., Bennett, L., Poundstone, C. C., Rice, M. E., Faibisch, F. M., Hunt, B., & Mitchell, A. (1996). Growth of literacy engagement: Changes in motivations and strategies during concept-oriented reading instruction. *Reading Research Quarterly, 31*, 306–332.
11. Pressley, M., El-Dinary, P. B., Brown, R., Schuder, T. L., Pioli, M., Green, K., & Gaskins, I. (1994). Transactional instruction of reading comprehension strategies. *Reading and Writing Quarterly, 10*, 5–19.
12. Reinking, D., & Watkins, J. (1997). *A formative experiment investigating the use of multimedia book reviews to increase elementary students' independent reading* (Reading Research Report No. 73). Athens, GA: Universities of Georgia and Maryland, National Reading Research Center.
13. Rosenblatt, L. M. (1985). Viewpoints: Transaction versus interaction—A terminological rescue operation. *Research in the Teaching of English, 19*(1), 96–107.
14. Roser, N. L., Hoffman, J. V., & Farest, C. (1990). Language, literature, and at-risk children. *Reading Teacher, 43*(8), 554–559.
15. Holdaway, C. (1979). *Foundations of literacy*. Portsmouth, NH: Heinemann.
16. Raphael, T., & McMahon, S. I. (1994). Book club: An alternative framework for reading instruction. *The Reading Teacher, 48*(2), 102–116.
17. Shockley, B., Michalove, B., & Allen, J. (1995). *Creating parallel practices: A home-to-school and school-to-home partnership* (Instructional Resource No. 13). Athens, GA: Universities of Georgia and Maryland, National Reading Research Center.
18. Veatch, J. (1960). In defense of individualized instruction. *Elementary English*, p. 227.
19. Stauffer, R. G. (1970). *The language experience approach to the teaching of reading*. New York: Harper Row.
20. Barbe, W. (1961). *Personalized reading*, Englewood Cliffs, NJ: Prentice-Hall.
21. Atwell, N. (1987). *In the middle: Writing, reading, and learning with adolescents*. Portsmouth, NH: Heinemann.
22. Price, D. (1998). Explicit instruction at the point of use. *Language Arts, 76*(1), 19–26.
23. Pauk, W. ((1993). *How to study in college.* (5th ed.). Boston.
24. Stauffer, R. G. (1969). *Directing reading maturity as a cognitive process*. New York: Harper Row.
25. Duffy, G. G., & Roehler, L. R. (1989). Improving classroom reading instruction: A decision-making approach. New York: Random House.
26. Ogle, D. (1986). The K-W-L: A teaching model that develops active reading of expository text. *The Reading Teacher, 39*, 564–576.
27. Hoffman, J. V. (1992). Critical reading/thinking across the curriculum: Using I-Charts to support learning. *Language Arts, 69*, 121–127.
28. Simpson, A. Critical questions: Whose questions? *Reading Teacher, 50*(2), 118–127.
29. Au, K. (1980). Participation structures in a reading lesson with Hawaiian children: Analysis of a culturally appropriate instructional event. *Anthropology and Education Quarterly, 9*(2), 91–115.
30. Ada, A. (1993). A critical pedagogy approach to fostering the home–school connection. *ERIC*: ED358716.
31. Moll, L., & Gonzalez, N. (1994). Lessons from research with language-minority children. *Journal of Reading Behavior, 26*(4), 99439–99456.

32. Ladson Billings, G. (1994). *The dream-keepers: Successful teachers of African-American children.* San Francisco: Jossey-Bass.
33. Sticht, T. (1977). Comprehending reading at work. In M. A. Just & P. A. Carpenter (Eds.), *Cognitive processes in comprehension.* Hillsdale, NJ: Lawrence Erlbaum Associates.
34. Kammann, M. R. (1975). The comprehensibility of printed instructions and the flowchart alternative. *Human Factors, 17,* 90–113.
35. Frierre, P. (1985). Reading the world and reading the word: An interview with Paulo Frieire. *Language Arts, 62,* 15–21.
36. Halliday, M. K. (1975). *Learning how to mean: Explorations in the development of language.* New York: Elsevier North Holland.
37. Huntley-Johnson, L., Merritt, S., & Huffman, L. (1997). How to do how-to books: Real-life writing in the classroom. *Journal of Adolescent & Adult Literacy, 41*(3), 172–179.
38. Paris, S. G., Cross, D. R., & Lipson, M. Y. (1983). Informed strategies for learning: A program to improve children's reading awareness and comprehension. *Journal of Educational Psychology, 76,* 1239–1252.
39. Duffy, G. G., & Roehler, L. R. (1989). *Improving classroom reading instruction: A decision-making approach.* New York: Random House.
40. Palinsar, A. S., & Brown, A. (1984). Reciprocal teaching of comprehension-fostering and comprehension-monitoring activities. *Cognition and Instruction, 1,* 117–175.
41. Stevens, R. J., Madden, N. A., Slavin, R. E., & Farnish, A. M. (1987). Cooperative integrated reading and composition: Two field experiments. *Reading Research Quarterly, 22,* 433–454.
42. Langer, J. A., & Applebee, A. N. (1986). Reading and writing instruction: Toward a theory of teaching and learning. In E. Rothkopf (Ed.), *Review of research in education* (Vol. 13, pp. 171–194). Washington, DC: American Educational Research Association.
43. Galda, L., Shockley, B., & Pellegrini, A. (1995). *Talking to read and write: Opportunities for literate talk in one primary classroom* (Instructional Resource No. 12). Athens, GA: Universities of Georgia and Maryland, National Reading Research Center.
44. Commeryras, M., & Sumner, G. (1995). Questions children want to discuss about literature: What teachers and students learned in a second-grade classroom. Reading Research Report No. 47. ED390031.
45. Goodman, Y., & Marek, A. (1996). *Retrospective miscue analysis.* New York: R.C. Owen.
46. Valencia, S. W., & Au, K. (1996). Portfolios across educational contexts: Issues of evaluation, teacher development, and system validity (Research Report No. 73). Athens, GA: Universities of Georgia and Maryland, National Reading Research Center.
47. Hoffman, J. V., Worthy, J., Roser, R., McKool, S., Rutherford, W., & Strecker, S. (1996). Performance assessment in first grade classrooms: *The PALM model* (Yearbook of the National Reading Conference). Chicago: National Reading Conference.

# III

# Our Past and Our Present

James F. Baumann
*University of Georgia*

Ann M. Duffy-Hester
*University of North Carolina at Greensboro*

Jennifer Moon Ro
*University of Georgia*

James V. Hoffman
*The University of Texas at Austin*

In the preceding part, we presented theoretically and empirically based principles for balanced reading instruction. In this part, we examine these principles in relation to historical and contemporary practices. We do so by presenting selected results of a modified replication of a classic study and by juxtaposing past and contemporary practices to the principles presented in Part II.

In 1963, Austin and Morrison published an influential research report, *The First R: The Harvard Report on Reading in Elementary Schools*,[1] in which they examined the status of reading instruction and achievement in U.S. elementary schools. Austin and Morrison found a static environment with little innovation, lamenting that recommendations expressed by reading authorities of the day were rarely heeded or evident in U.S. elementary classrooms. The authors concluded that "the results of the present Harvard-Carnegie study indicate that the teaching of reading in the elementary schools today is mediocre at best" (p. 235).[2]

We recently conducted a modified replication of Austin and Morrison's *The First R*, surveying contemporary U.S. elementary teachers and administrators regarding their reading instruction philosophies and practices.[3] What did we find? How do practices today compare to those of yesterday? Are current practices in elementary reading instruction compatible or discordant with our nine principles? Do contemporary practices promote balance or equilibrium among the readers' goals, reading context demands, and readers' abilities?

We address these questions by first providing a brief description of the original *First R* study and our modified replication of it. Next, we present an overview of the results of our survey, contrasting them to Austin and Morrison's findings. We then discuss in greater detail what we learned about contemporary reading instruction practices and philosophies in relation to our nine principles. We conclude by reflecting on the degree to which modern instruction supports learners' ability to engage in truly balanced reading and by considering implications of our comparisons between elementary reading instruction of yesterday and today.

## THE ORIGINAL *FIRST R* STUDY AND A MODIFIED REPLICATION

Austin and Morrison began their exploration of reading instruction in *The Torchlighters: Tomorrow's Teachers of Reading*,[4] their 1961 book in which they investigated elementary teacher education programs in U.S. colleges and universities. From this study, they concluded that prospective teachers of reading were not always adequately prepared to help children learn to read, which led them to explore the nature of reading instruction in U.S. elementary schools. In their follow-up study, *The First R*, Austin and Morrison used mail questionnaires to query administrators in 1,023 U.S. school districts about the content and conduct of Kindergarten through Grade 6 reading instruction. They also visited 65 school systems in which they observed lessons in elementary classrooms and interviewed teachers, principals, and central office personnel.

Austin and Morrison's overall conclusion was that elementary school reading programs were substandard in general and were not capable of preparing students for future literacy demands. They identified five general areas they believed demanded the greatest and most urgent improvement: "(1) a challenging developmental program for all children; (2) better provision for individual differences; (3) more stimulating programs for the gifted reader; (4) improved teacher preparation; and (5) more effective leadership at the administrative level" (p. 3).[5] The authors then presented 45 specific recommendations that addressed these broad areas.

In our modified replication of Austin and Morrison's *The First R*, we queried teachers and administrators through three mail surveys: (a) the Teacher Survey, which was distributed to a national random sample of Prekindergarten through Grade 5 elementary teachers; (b) the Building Administrator Survey, which went to a sample of elementary school principals and assistant principals; and (c) the District Administrator Survey, which was distributed to a central-office administrator responsible for reading instruction. The surveys were modeled after original *First R* documents but were adapted to include issues and topics relevant to contemporary elementary reading teachers. Responses were received from 1,207 elementary classroom teachers, 161 building administrators of schools in which some of these teachers worked, and 48 district administrators in school systems in which some of these teachers and building administrators worked.

## READING INSTRUCTION TODAY VIS-À-VIS YESTERDAY

Table 3.1 presents a summary of the results from our survey, juxtaposed to findings reported by Austin and Morrison. This comparison between elementary reading instruction in 1961, when data were gathered, and now reveals both commonality and divergence regarding philosophy and practices.

### Differences in Reading Instruction: Then and Now

There are several features that distinguish reading instruction practices today from those of 1961. Contemporary public elementary school teachers have more professional education than their predecessors, and the student population is much more culturally diverse than it was in the 1960s. Teachers today embrace a balanced, eclectic philosophy, as opposed to a heavy skills-based perspective in the past. Although this is not exactly balance in the sense of equilibrium within the reader, we find the movement toward curriculum and instruction that provide learners both explicit skill and strategy instruction and many literacy immersion activities to be generally compatible with the internal balance notion.

Related to the balance notion, teachers today tend to blend the use of trade books and basals, as opposed to basal-only usage in the past. An emergent literacy framework has replaced a reading readiness perspective, and phonics tends to be taught synthetically today versus analytically in the past. Whole-class instruction seems to have supplanted ability grouping as the primary structure for reading instruction, and teachers are much more likely to employ informal or alternative assessments today than their 1960s counterparts. Teachers today report greater programmatic support for struggling readers than teachers of yesterday. School and classroom libraries are common and generally well equipped today, as opposed to the infrequent or poorly stocked school libraries of the past. Teachers and administrators tend to share decision making about the reading program in the 1990s, unlike the

TABLE 3.1

Summary of Survey Findings: Today and Yesteryear

| Category | Current Findings | 1961 *First R* Findings |
|---|---|---|
| Overall profile of teachers and schools | • Educated, experienced, professionally active workforce | • Administrators read professional journals |
| | • Diverse children in varied districts | • Few teachers with advanced degrees |
| | • Presence of teacher research | • Presence of "action research" |
| | • Lukewarm evaluation of preservice courses in teaching reading | • General dissatisfaction with preservice courses in teaching reading |
| Philosophy and goals | • Balanced, eclectic perspective pervaded | • Heavy reliance on basal materials suggested a skills-based perspective |
| | • Major theme of systematic instruction in decoding along with a literature-rich environment | • Teachers promoted independent, self-selected reading |
| | • Common goal was to produce skillful, fluent, motivated, independent readers | • Phonics taught along with other word identification skills |
| Instructional time and materials | • Considerable time dedicated to reading and language arts instruction and activities | • Considerable time dedicated to teaching reading skills |
| | • Basals and trade books used in combination | • High reliance on basals, with infrequent use of trade books |

| | | |
|---|---|---|
| Beginning reading instruction | • Emergent literacy perspective commonly held | •Reading readiness framework assumed |
| | • Synthetic phonics taught directly and systematically | • Formal reading instruction deferred until students deemed ready through readiness tests |
| | • Multiple word identification skills taught in context-rich ways | • Phonics taught analytically through basal materials |
| | • High incidence of reading aloud, exposure to literature, and independent, self-selected reading | • Dissatisfaction with content of basal selections |
| Organizing for instruction | • Students typically assigned heterogeneously to self-contained classrooms | • Students typically assigned heterogeneously to self-contained classrooms |
| | • Whole-class reading instruction common with some flexible grouping | • Ability groups predominate for reading instruction |
| Reading assessment | • Teachers commonly used alternative assessment measures and procedures | • Standardized tests administered almost universally but utilized very little |
| | • Standardized tests still mandated and administered | • Basal tests used occasionally |
| | • Teachers report alternative assessments useful; administrators reported standardized tests useful | • Informal tests used infrequently |

(continued on next page)

| | | |
|---|---|---|
| Teaching struggling and gifted readers | • Classroom teachers expected to accommodate struggling and gifted readers | • Modest classroom and programmatic support for struggling readers |
| | • Special support programs or teachers for struggling readers generally available, but less often for gifted readers | • Infrequent or poor programs for gifted readers |
| Libraries and leadership | • Strong school libraries and frequent in-classroom libraries | • School and in-classroom libraries less frequent and evaluated poorly |
| | • Teachers and administrators share decision-making about reading programs | • Program decisions typically made by school or district administrators with little teacher involvement |
| | • Modest amount of district-sponsored in-service programs | • Sporadic inservice programs of dubious quality |
| Changes and challenges | • Changes and innovations in reading programs common | • Changes and innovations not very prevalent |
| | • Most common changes: adoption of a new philosophy or program (often literature-based) and accommodating struggling readers | • Most common changes: materials selection and organization plans |
| | • Greatest challenges: accommodating struggling readers and lack of support (parent, administrative, funding) for reading programs | • Greatest challenge: dealing with "underachieving reader" the pervasive issue |
| | • Enhanced teacher knowledge and professional development a significant need in eyes of administrators | |

top–down, administrator-only decision making process of the past. In-service programs are more systematic and widespread today than they were in the past, and educational changes and innovations—rare phenomena in the 1960s—are the norm in classrooms, schools, and districts in the 1990s. In sum, it is clear that the school environment with respect to reading instruction has changed significantly over the past 35 years.

## Similarities in Reading Instruction: Then and Now

But not all has changed, for there remain a number of commonalities between the face of reading instruction today and that of the 1960s. The contemporary movement toward classroom-based, teacher research is paralleled by the action research Austin and Morrison reported in the 1960s. Teachers in 1961 were generally displeased with their preprofessional training in reading instruction, and teachers today rated their preparation to teach reading and language arts as only adequate. Teachers today dedicate considerable amounts of time to reading instruction as did their 1960s counterparts. Phonics is being taught to beginning readers today just as it was in the past, although the specific approach for such instruction may differ somewhat. Standardized reading tests are still mandated and administered today, just as they were in 1961. Teachers today remain dissatisfied with programs for gifted readers, as did their predecessors. Although the labels and descriptions may have changed, teachers and administrators today view accommodating struggling readers to be a major challenge, a worry likewise expressed by administrators and teachers in 1961. And enhanced teacher knowledge and professional development about reading remains a major concern for administrators today, mirroring a lament noted by Austin and Morrison over 35 years ago.

In conclusion, although changes between the 1960s and 1990s are obvious and significant, there remain a number of issues and concerns to contemporary educators that uncannily parallel those of the past.

## PRINCIPLES VERSUS PRACTICE

We now turn to the issue of the compatibility between the reading instructional principles presented in Part II of this book and the actual practices revealed through our *First R* modified replication. The former describe an empirically and theoretically based conception of reading instruction in which children develop into mature, independent readers, that is, an *ideal* type of reading program. The latter involve what we learned from our surveys about the actual nature of contemporary elementary reading instruction, that is, the *real* reading programs children are experiencing in the 1990s. Table 3.2 lists the nine principles nested within the three components of the model of independence in reading presented in Part II. We structure our data presentation and discussion that follows by examining the degree to which current practices in reading instruction match the nine principles.

TABLE 3.2

Match Between the Model of Independence in Reading and Elementary
Teachers' and Administrators' Reports of Current Reading Practices

| | Compliance to model of independence in reading | | |
| Principle | High | Moderate | Low |
|---|---|---|---|
| Component I: Independent Readers Apply Skills and Strategies to Access Text | | | |
| 1. Independent readers are automatic in word recognition. | ◆ | | |
| 2. Independent readers are fluent in processing text. | ◆ | | |
| 3. Independent readers are flexible in adapting to purpose and text structure. | | | ◆ |
| Component II: Independent Readers Seek Meaning | | | |
| 4. Independent readers seek experiences through text. | | ◆ | |
| 5. Independent readers seek to develop new knowledge through text. | | ◆ | |
| 6. Independent readers seek guidance and direction through text experiences. | | | ◆ |
| Component III: Independent Readers Self Monitor | | | |
| 7. Independent readers self-monitor the process of reading. | | ◆ | |
| 8. Independent readers self-monitor the products of their reading. | | ◆———◆ | |
| 9. Independent readers self-monitoring their progress and development | | ◆———◆ | |

# Component I: Independent Readers Apply Skills and Strategies to Access Text

Component I includes Principles 1 through 3, which deal with skills and strategies readers must acquire to achieve automaticity in word recognition, fluency
in text processing, and the ability to adapt strategies to the text structure and
reading purpose. Overall, reading programs implemented by elementary
teachers and administrators in the 1990s demonstrate High degrees of compatibility with Principles 1 and 2 but Low compatibility with Principle 3.

Teachers and administrators were clear in expressing their value for the development of children who were skillful and strategic. When presented with various goal statements, 88% of Prekindergarten through Grade 5 teachers, 96% of building administrators, and 100% of district administrators indicated that it was their goal "to develop readers who were skillful and strategic in word identification, fluency, and reading comprehension." Additionally, teachers provided time for teaching reading skills and strategies. Of the average 2 hours and 23 minutes total that elementary teachers devoted daily to reading and language arts, 55 minutes were dedicated to teacher-directed reading skills or strategy instruction, which was described as "reading 'groups,' skill or strategy lessons, teacher-guided reading of selections, etc."

When asked about the importance of decoding instruction, 63% of Prekindergarten through Grade 5 teachers selected the statement, "I believe that phonics needs to be taught directly to beginning readers in order for students to become fluent, skillful readers," as representative of their philosophical perspective. When we queried those teachers directly responsible for developing word recognition skills in beginning readers, they were even more emphatic about the importance of decoding instruction. Ninety-nine percent of Kindergarten through Grade 3 teachers indicated that "teaching phonic analysis skills/strategies" was "Essential" (67%) or "Important" (32%), with only 0.6% indicating that such instruction was "Not Important." It was also clear that phonics instruction was systematic, with 66% of Kindergarten through Grade 2 teachers indicating that they employed "synthetic phonics (systematic instruction in which students are taught letter/sound correspondences first and then are taught how to decode words)." Another significant proportion (40%) indicated that they also taught "analytic phonics (systematic instruction in which students are taught some sight words first and then are taught phonics generalizations from these words)." Only 19% indicated that phonics was taught "only as needed (not systematic instruction; rather, students are taught phonic analysis skills as the need arises)."

Kindergarten through Grade 2 teachers were varied and inventive in their phonics instruction, with approximately two thirds indicating that they taught phonics "by way of word families or phonograms" (66%), "in the context of literature" (62%), and "in the context of writing and spelling" (73%). But Kindergarten through Grade 2 teachers balanced phonics instruction with other word identification strategies, for significant majorities indicated that it was "Essential" or "Important" for teachers to provide supportive word-reading skills that included instruction in contextual analysis (99%), structural analysis (93%), and sight vocabulary (96%). Thus, there is evidence that teachers practiced what they preached when it came to teaching students to read words automatically, fluently, and in the context of authentic reading situations (Principles 1–2).

There is less evidence, however, that reading programs emphasized teaching students to adapt their reading to varying purposes and text structures (Principle 3). Our surveys did not explore teachers' adaptive reading structures, so we cannot evaluate that program aspect, but the surveys did inquire about the use of various texts and instruction about them. Although about three fourths of administrators indicated that it was their "goal to developed readers who are knowledgeable about literary forms or genres and about different text types or structures," only a little more than half (57%) of the teachers identified this as an instructional goal. And when we asked Grades 3 through 5 teachers whether "reading nonfiction trade books in order to learn about expository genres" was a regular part of their classroom program, only 41% indicated that it was. Thus, there is indication that teachers might do more to provide students exposure and instruction to adapt their reading to varying purposes and text characteristics.

## Component II: Independent Readers Seek Meaning

Component II includes Principles 4 through 6, which deal with how readers seek meaning from text through various aesthetic experiences and interpretations, by learning from textual information, and by engaging with texts that provide guidance and direction. Overall, reading programs of today demonstrate Moderate compatibility with Principles 4 and 5 but Low compatibility with Principle 6.

Regarding how teachers promoted students' aesthetic experiences with text (Principle 4), there was strong agreement (94% of teachers, 96% of building administrators, 92% of district administrators) with the statement, "It is my goal to develop readers who are independent and motivated to choose, appreciate, and enjoy literature." Furthermore, 71% of teachers selected the statement, "I believe students need to be immersed in literature and literacy experiences in order to become fluent readers," as being representative of their beliefs.

These beliefs appear to have some support in practice. Teachers dedicated an average of 42 minutes daily for applying, modeling, and practicing reading abilities ("reading aloud to children, students' independent reading or DEAR periods, student-led response groups, cooperative reading activities, etc."), with 46 more minutes each day reserved for language arts activities ("writing workshop, response journals, spelling, oral language activities, etc."). Ninety-three percent of Prekindergarten through Grade 5 teachers reported allocating Moderate (49%) or Considerable (44%) amounts of time to reading aloud to children. Furthermore, 69% of Prekindergarten through Grade 2 teachers indicated that they engaged "regularly" (defined as "3 or more times per week") in reading response activities. It seems, therefore, that teachers valued and dedicated time for aesthetic activities.

In contrast, only about half of Prekindergarten through Grade 2 teachers (55%) and Grades 3 through 5 teachers (54%) reported engaging in Reading Workshop "regularly" (3+ times per week), and less than half of the Prekindergarten through Grade 2 teachers (42%) and Grades 3 through 5 teachers (38%) reported using some form of Reading Workshop on a "regular" basis. Furthermore, when asked about how much time was dedicated to the use of "Literature Circles, Book Clubs, literature discussion groups," 64% of Prekindergarten through Grade 5 teachers reported dedicating "Little" (38%)

or "None" (26%), and only 25% of teachers at Grades 3 through 5 indicated that they engaged students in literature discussion groups "regularly." Thus, teachers expressed the importance of engaging students in aesthetic reading activities and experiences and appear to set aside time for them, but there was some evidence that they actually did not engage students in such activities regularly.

There was a similar pattern regarding data on teaching students to acquire new knowledge through text (Principle 5). Ninety-seven percent of Prekindergarten through Grade 5 teachers indicated that they dedicated "Considerable" (67%) or "Moderate" (30%) instructional time to teaching reading comprehension, and 85% indicated that they dedicated "Considerable" (34%) or "Moderate" (51%) instructional time to teaching reading vocabulary. When we asked Grades 3 through 5 teachers about their instructional emphases, 89% indicated that they engaged in comprehension strategy instruction "regularly" (3+ times per week), and 80% indicated that vocabulary lessons were regular occurrences. Overall, teachers reported "Moderate" use of nonfiction trade books in their classrooms, and they also indicated that they "Sometimes" or "Often" used "trade books to support content area studies in science, social studies, and mathematics." However, only slightly more than half of Grades 3 through 5 teachers indicated that they "regularly" engaged in teaching strategies along with content subjects (58%) or critical reading lessons or activities (54%). This suggests that although teachers expended considerable effort in teaching reading comprehension and vocabulary skills and strategies, they seemed not to extend this instruction with equivalent vigor when it came to learning information from text or responding to it critically.

Regarding critical reading, another aspect of Principle 5, surveys revealed that over 90% of administrators and over 75% of teachers agreed that "it is my goal to develop readers who are critical and thoughtful in using reading and writing to learn about people and ideas, and how they might use literacy to positively affect the world in which they live." Three fourths of Prekindergarten through Grade 5 teachers reported dedicating "Moderate" or "Considerable" amounts of instructional time to critical reading activities; however, only about half of Grades 3 through 5 teachers indicated that "critical reading lessons or activities" were regular parts of their curriculum. These findings suggest that administrators and teachers see the importance of promoting children's critical reading and that efforts are being made to promote these abilities, although teachers' instructional emphases may not be quite commensurate with their values.

Regarding Principle 6, our surveys did not directly explore the manner in which the reading curriculum and instruction dealt with procedural or "how-to" texts. As noted previously, there was strong support among administrators and moderate support among teachers for the goal of developing readers who are knowledgeable about various literary forms, genres, and text structures, suggesting that there may be support for teaching students to grapple with "how to" texts. On the other hand, upper elementary teachers reported infrequent use of nonfiction trade books to learn about informational text genres, so students may not be provided exposure and instruction to materials that are likely to contain procedural texts. This conjecture is supported by teachers' reports about the usage of other literacy curricular materials. Although many teachers reported that nonfiction trade books were incorporated into their instructional programs, other materials that are likely to include procedural texts were used instructionally less frequently. Specifically, 59% of teachers reported "Moderate" or greater use of computer hardware and software in their classrooms, and only 41% reported "Moderate" or greater use of magazines and newspapers. Thus, it is our estimate that there is a Low degree of match between current practices and Principle 6.

## Component III: Independent Readers Self-Monitor

Component III includes principles which involve teaching and guiding students to self-monitor the process of reading, to monitor the products of reading, and to reflect on their reading progress and development. Overall, reading programs of today demonstrate Moderate compatibility with Principle 7 and Moderate to Low compatibility with Principles 8 and 9.

Although our survey did not probe respondents extensively about teachers' efforts to teach students to self-monitor the reading process, the data we have suggest that teachers addressed this area to a certain extent. There was almost universal agreement about the importance of developing readers who are skillful and strategic in reading comprehension, and more than ample instructional time was dedicated to comprehension instruction. We presume that teachers incorporated aspects of comprehension monitoring and fix-up strategies into their reading comprehension instructional programs. Additionally, 71% of teachers in Grades 3 through 5 indicated that they regularly provided students "instruction in comprehension monitoring (e.g., self-questioning, applying 'fix-up' strategies such as rereading)." Thus, we determined that current practices indicate Moderate compatibility with Principle 7.

Principles 8 and 9 address assessment aspects of the reading program, the former involving teaching students to monitor and evaluate their reading and writing products and the latter involving teaching students to monitor and assess their reading development. Our results revealed that the majority of elementary teachers today are embracing alternative assessments. About one fifth (21%) of teachers indicated that they "rely extensively on alternative reading assessments", another third (31%) noted that they were "moving toward adopting various forms of alternative reading assessments", and still another third (33%) indicated that they used "a mix of conventional assessment measures … and some informal assessments."

In spite of teachers' movement toward alternative assessments, the surveys provide little insight into how students monitor the reading products or reading development. Teachers did report employing various informal and alternative assessments. Specifically, when asked, "To what degree do you use results from the following types of assessments to make instructional decisions in your class-room?", teachers responded to a 4-point scale (*Considerable* = 4, *Moderate* = 3, *Little* = 2, *None* = 1) indicating that the most useful tools for instructional decision making included reading/writing portfolios ($m$ = 2.9), observational checklists/anecdotal records ($m$ = 2.8), and running records ($m$ = 2.6). We expect that teachers who adopt an alternative assessment philosophy and employ procedures like the preceding—a portfolio approach in particular—invite students to monitor their reading products and development, perhaps modeling for them how to do so. However, this speculation would be needed to be verified through subsequent research, so at this point we judge current practices in relation to Principles 8 and 9 to be in the Moderate to Low range.

In summary, teachers of the 1990s, as evidenced by their reported instructional philosophy and actions, embrace overall the contemporary model of elementary reading instruction as outlined in Part II of this book. This is certainly true with regard to their efforts to promote students' skills and strategies for decoding words and reading text independently and fluently, and there is some evidence, albeit less compelling, that contemporary teachers likewise promote students' meaning acquisition and self-monitoring behaviors.

## BALANCED READING: LIP-SERVICE OR REALITY?

Our survey data indicate that teachers and administrators clearly espoused a balanced reading perspective. They aligned themselves with an "eclectic" philosophy and expressed that skill and strategy instruction was balanced by engagement with whole texts and language-rich activities. This conception of curricular and instructional balance is compatible with recent descriptions of balance between holistic teaching and more traditional skill-based learning.[6] We have characterized this type of contemporary reading instruction as *disciplined eclecticism*:

> The majority of U.S. public school elementary teachers do *not* assume polar or extreme positions when it comes to reading and language arts pedagogy. They neither teach phonics to the exclusion of providing children enriched literacy instruction nor immerse students in holistic literacy experiences devoid of reading skill instruction. Instead, we found that teachers design reading and language arts programs that provide children with a multi-faceted, balanced instructional diet that includes an artful blend of direct instruction in phonics and other reading and writing strategies along with a rich assortment of literature, oral language, and written language experiences and activities. (p. 646)[7]

Is this popular conception of balance the kind of balance that involves internal equilibrium within the learner? Yes and no. Our response is *no* in the sense in that the survey questions we asked did not directly probe teachers' beliefs about developing in their students a kind of literacy homeostasis, that is, a literacy that integrates the goals, demands, and abilities required for mature, independent reading. Thus, we have no direct evidence that teachers are adopting a kind of Piagetian stance toward balance.

But we also respond with a qualified *yes* in the sense that our survey responses suggest a value for and movement toward literacy equilibrium. Not only did teachers and administrators express a value for eclecticism, they demonstrated a sensitivity to understanding varying reader goals (e.g., implementation of alternative assessment measures and procedures), adjusting to different reading contexts (e.g., teaching reading skill lessons, providing opportunities to practice developing literacy abilities, encouraging literacy activities in the home), and accommodating readers' diverse abilities (e.g., concern for accommodating struggling and accelerated readers). Thus, we see more and more teachers and administrators today demonstrating a kind of tacit understanding of the importance of promoting an internal literacy equilibrium in their students. As a result, we envision a kind of neo-balanced view of literacy emerging that is captured quite well by Spiegel's definition: "A balanced approach to literacy development is a decision-making approach through which the teacher makes thoughtful choices each day about the best way to help each child become a better reader and writer" (p. 116).[8]

## "WILL TOMORROW BE ANOTHER DAY?"

Drawing from the reading education literature of the time, Austin and Morrison provided their research team a checklist of evidence they considered essential for a successful reading program.[9] This enabled them to compare the actual performance of district reading programs to the ideal, as determined by their research- and theory-based checklist. After making visits to many school districts that involved interviews and observations, the research team determined the effectiveness of the reading programs to be "good" in 33% of the districts, "fair" in 51%, and "poor" in 16% (p. 2).[10] In other words, Austin and Morrison judged that the implementation and application of reading programs and instruction in the early 1960s was substandard in two thirds of the districts they examined closely. Their conclusion was "that present-day reading programs were mediocre at best and not currently designed to produce a future society of *mature* readers" (p. 2).[11]

In their final chapter of *The First R*, which was titled "Will Tomorrow Be Another Day?", Austin and Morrison's admonished educators of the 1960s that they should refrain from being complacent in their work and provide citizens reading instruction that accommodates both present and future needs.[12] They then listed 45 recommendations that they believed, if adopted, would remedy the "mediocre" state of reading instruction at that time.

Our evaluation is parallel in process to *The First R* in that we too have compared the actual with the ideal. We established a set of nine empirically and theoretically based principles that distinguish sound, balanced reading instruction, that is, the ideal, and compared these principles to the actual, our survey data. Unlike Austin and Morrison, however, we did not find large-scale discrepancies between the actual and the ideal (see Table 3.2). Indeed there remains much work to improve U.S. elementary reading instruction to provide more children higher levels of achievement, but current practices are promising and we are optimistic about the future. We are encouraged by the sensible, neo-balanced philosophy that teachers embrace today and by the major innovations and changes teachers and administrators are exploring in their districts, schools, and classrooms. [13]

Our surveys suggest great energy in classrooms and administrators' offices; a commitment to children, teaching, and learning; and a desire to move elementary reading instruction forward in spite of the many challenges public educators face. We did not find complacency but rather a sense of motivated urgency to move instructional principles, practices, and philosophies forward to accommodate the learners of the third millennium. We now move in the final section of this book to a discussion of how elementary educators might transform today's reading instruction into a form appropriate for "another day," that is, a reading program responsive to children of the 21st century.

## NOTES

1. Austin, M. C., & Morrison, C., with Morrison. M. B., Sipay, E. R., Gutmann, A. R., Torrant, K. E., & Woodbury, C. A. (1963). *The first R: The Harvard report on reading in elementary schools.* New York: Macmillan.
2. Austin & Morrison, 1963, p. 235.
3. Baumann, J. F., Hoffman, J. V., Duffy-Hester, A. M., & Moon, J. S. (in press). *The First R yesterday and today: U.S. elementary reading instruction practices reported by teachers and administrators. Reading Research Quarterly.*
4. Austin, M. C., Morrison, C., Kenney, H. J., Morrison, M. B., Gutmann, A. R., & Nystrom, J. W. (1961). *The torchlighters: Tomorrow's teachers of reading.* Cambridge, MA: Harvard University Press.
5. Austin & Morrison, 1963, p. 3.
6. McIntyre, E., & Pressley, M. (Eds.). (1996). *Balanced instruction: Strategies and skills in whole language.* Norwood, MA: Christopher-Gordon.
Reutzel, D. R., & Cooter, R. B. (1999). *Balanced reading strategies and practices: Assessing and assisting readers with special needs.* Upper Saddle River, NJ: Prentice-Hall.
7. Baumann, J. F., Hoffman, J. V., Moon, J., & Duffy-Hester, A. M. (1998). Where are teachers' voices in the phonics/whole language debate? Results from a survey of U.S. elementary classroom teachers. *The Reading Teacher, 51,* 636–650.
8. Spiegel, D. L. (1998). Silver bullets, babies, and bath water: Literature response groups in a balanced literacy program. *The Reading Teacher, 52,* 114–124.
9. Austin & Morrison, 1963, p. x.
10. Austin & Morrison, 1963, p. 2.
11. Austin & Morrison, 1963, p. 2.
12. Austin & Morrison, 1963, p. 218
13. Responses to open-ended questions in the surveys indicated that teachers and administrators were actively engaging in many, significant changes and innovations in reading curriculum and instruction, quite unlike the rather static state Austin and Morrison reported in 1963. See Baumann et al. (in press) for details.

# IV

# Our Plans and Our Future

Peter Afflerbach
*The University of Maryland*

*Make haste slowly.*

—Abraham Lincoln

In this final part we examine the ways and means of improving reading instruction, and the centrality of teachers' professional development to students' learning to be better readers. We revisit the importance of research and reflection that are described earlier in this volume. Next, we examine the characteristics of strategic change in successful reading programs. We provide a blueprint for an action agenda that initiates and sustains both effective reading programs and teachers' professional development. Our goal is to describe how the knowledge we possess about reading and teaching can be used to effect balance in children's lives as readers.

We begin this part with a sense of urgency and a sense of optimism. There is the need to act quickly with an informed plan to help elementary school students become successful readers. Although many children learn to read, too many do not.[1] We know that behind headlines laced with doom and vitriol are students, students who want the wonder of creativity, the nourishment of character, and the opportunities for achievement that reading provides. Teaching these students is a corps of dedicated professionals who seek to meet the needs of all students. For these students and their teachers, reading and the teaching of reading are keys to the future. Despite the best of intentions, some students do not learn to read. Nor do they learn to value reading. This lack of reading accomplishment occurs at a time when society is becoming increasingly information oriented. The types and amount of information that may help elementary school students more fully develop their personal and professional lives are rapidly expanding. The meteoric rise of the use of the internet and the accelerating loss of blue collar jobs both point to a future that will demand that children develop specialized literacy skills for personal success. Reading is central to the future, and lack of reading ability will lead to lives that are less rich and less rewarding for many children.

We choose to meet this urgent situation with optimism. Our optimism springs from three sources. First, there is an increasingly diverse array of reading research and related results that can inform classroom practice. The focus, form, and content of this reading inquiry is informed by many disciplines, as portrayed in Part II. In addition, the diversity of participants in reading research and the roles they play in inquiry are expanding. Reading research is more inclusive. The result is a reading research base that is more relevant and accessible to classroom practitioners. This research can inform different initiatives, such as the development of effective reading instruction methods and materials, the building of school, home, and community collaborations, and the creation of useful reading assessments. A second source of optimism is the existing catalog of proven instructional and organizational practices, structures, and systems that can help us meet the goal of improved reading for the diversity of students in today's reading classroom. Around the country, there are reading success stories to be told by students, teachers, parents, and administrators. Reading improvement, teaching improvement, and school improvement share common ground, and each can inform the other. Some of these success stories are described in Part III, our account of the replication of *The First R*. The third cause for optimism is that there are promising professional development opportunities that can enhance the efforts of teachers and administrators as they try to better reading instruction and learning. We are firm in our belief that student success in reading is the result of talented teaching. Successful schools are those that combine effective practice, appropriate materials, and continual professional development for teachers.

It is our hope that this volume informs the process by which schools examine their existing reading programs and enact positive change. In this final part, then, we will revisit reading research and consider how it enriches our understanding of reading and how to teach it. We then focus on the need for examination and reflection related to current reading instruction practice. We examine the questions included in the replication of *The First R* while considering the value of asking "What do we do?" and "Why do we do it?" as entry into examination of our professional practice. Next, we describe the characteristics of successful schools. We then overview promising programs that combine collaborative inquiry, teacher reflection, and discussion to enhance professional development and the teaching and learning of reading. We conclude with suggestions for creating an action agenda that might facilitate positive change in reading instruction and reading achievement.

We see parallels between the process we undertook to create this volume and the process a school might undertake to enhance or develop an effective reading program. A first parallel relates to the brief review of current reading research that was presented in Part I. Just as we collected and generated information and research results central to our task of building this book, teachers and schools must construct the knowledge that is relevant to their efforts and goals for school, classroom, and student. The sources that contribute to this constructed knowledge may be the results of careful teacher inquiry, of research published in refereed professional journals, or of engaging discussions of both. A second parallel relates to the accounting of current reading instruction practice. Earlier in this book we described the replication of *The First R* in which teachers and administrators were encouraged to engage in self-examination and self-evaluation. Similarly, schools and teachers must develop an accurate description of current reading instruction practice in order to determine existing strengths and challenges. We believe a survey of practice similar to that described in Part III enables careful accounting of what is done in schools and classrooms. In turn, this information can be used to determine if reading instruction is effective. We see a potential symbiosis in the two related processes of constructing research knowledge and examining practice: one may influence the other, and both may contribute to teachers' professional development. Combined, they place a school community in a good position for enacting positive change and the improvement of instruction and learning.

## THE USEFULNESS OF READING RESEARCH

Research can contribute to a change process that results in effective elementary reading programs and increased student reading achievement. This research may be outside-in, conducted by researchers whose work is disseminated to classroom teachers and reading program administrators. The research may be inside-out, conducted by teachers investigating their students and their practice. The research may be collaborative, as teachers consult a body of knowledge created by others. Or the research may be a second sort of collaborative effort that combines the interests and strengths of a group of teachers and researchers. Each approach requires that the teachers and researchers are empowered and supported. Moreover, they must be talented: skilled at framing questions pertinent to classroom practice, designing inquiry, collecting and analyzing classroom data, and discussing the process and content of research along the way. In all cases, a working knowledge of reading processes and contexts and of the varied influences on reading instruction and learning is crucial.

Earlier in this volume we became familiar with research that describes different facets of the act of reading. We believe that the teaching of reading can benefit from ideas and insights that are generated from research in diverse fields. These include cognitive psychology, developmental psychology, educational psychology, linguistics, sociology, and anthropology. Indeed, how we think about reading can be informed by this increasingly rich and complex knowledge base. This knowledge base helps us examine schools from a variety of perspectives, as reading research is conceptualized by researchers from outside and inside the classroom. A result is that we know a lot about the reading process, how children learn to be better readers, and how best to teach reading. We have the continuing opportunity to add to our knowledge in each of the three areas.

Understanding the factors that influence students' reading achievement can contribute to our teaching effectiveness, and research can enrich this understanding. For example, a common concern of the elementary school teachers who participated in *The First R* replication is how best to teach the diverse range of students found in almost every classroom. Here, knowledge of different reading research paradigms and traditions related to diverse students and the reading classroom can alert us to potential challenges and prepare us to meet those challenges. Heath[2] described diverse groups of young children who come to schools with quite different experiences, knowledge, and expectations related to reading. She suggested that our attention to these differences may ultimately enhance our teaching and increase student learning, for children's experiences and expectations may facilitate or hinder their progress in relation to the classroom culture. Moll et al[3] described funds of knowledge that may serve as common and instructionally fertile ground between students' lives outside of school and the reading curriculum constructed within their neighborhood school. Allington[4] examined the reading instruction given to good and poor readers (noting poor readers often get significantly fewer opportunities to read), and describes the importance of providing struggling readers with time to read engaging texts. Research also describes the importance of motivation, the range of motivations that readers may bring to the classroom,[5] and the influence of motivation on academic success. As children develop their reading ability, research can inform our means of teaching phonemic awareness[6] and comprehension,[7] as well as encouraging children's ongoing interpretation and response to literature.[8] As we contemplate this array of instruction, Delpit[9] suggested that children's "fit" with the classroom culture determines, in part, the type of instruction they may need to succeed. Descriptions of the school and community contexts in which diverse students learn also provide potentially valuable information.[10] In summary, a teacher's ability to construct an understanding of diverse students, their reading, and how best to teach them further may be enhanced by reading research information, as it is applied in relation to a particular classroom.

The reading research base is rich and potentially helpful: Knowing it can provide the teacher with resources that help make a difference in students' reading instruction and learning. Reading research can serve several important purposes as we examine existing reading programs and contemplate an action agenda for their maintenance or change. First, reading research results can be compared with our experiences, knowledge, and intuition. When research and personal experience converge, each supports and affirms the other. Relevant reading research can also help us question our intuition, reflect on our own practice, and inform our critical decision making. This can provide a level of confidence with which to undertake programmatic change, or to stand firm with established practice. Second, the careful examination and use of reading research can help us save time, a scarce commodity in school (another is money). There is something to be said for planning and teaching reading in relation to the seminal research that is critical to a classroom or school change plan. For example, research describes the value of discussion and dialog for social and cognitive growth in theoretical[11] and applied contexts.[12] Teachers may compare their own classrooms and practices with research findings to determine the suitability of processes and materials that prove successful in other classrooms. Many resources have been given to the investigation of what reading is, how reading works, and how best to teach it in elementary school classrooms. It should be fruitful to consult this considerable body of knowledge.

A third important contribution of research is that it may provide us with models of questions to ask, and models of the manner in which to answer these questions. How have researchers, including teachers and university professors, framed their inquiries? How have they chosen to "look" within the classroom and the intricacies of the reading lesson? What type of inquiry is most valuable for a particular teacher's purposes? Are researchers inside or outside the classroom asking questions that are similar to those that I ask about my students and my practice? With these and other questions, knowledge of the process and content of reading research is critical, even as it tells us that important questions (those determined by knowledgeable teachers of reading) remain to be asked. A fourth potential contribution of reading research is that it may provide a focus for discussions by school community members. When teachers meet regularly to discuss research that is pertinent to their students and their teaching, there is the opportunity to construct shared understandings of challenges and of possible solutions to the challenges. Discussions of research can lead us to consensus on what needs most attention, and how best to use our energies to attend to these needs.

We note that the historic separation of research and practice is unfortunate, and that the idea that one simply can take research results generated from classrooms removed in place and time from one's own is misguided. The models and mechanisms for "outside in" research having positive influences in classrooms still are often wanting. And as we sketch in the final section of this book, we note that some of the most effective and positive change in reading instruction may be facilitated by research that is conceptualized and conducted by capable teachers who are researchers. This allows for the construction of knowledge that is central to the needs of teachers and their students and for the more efficient use of research findings to inform and improve local practice.

## THE USEFULNESS OF SURVEYING AND EXAMINING CLASSROOM PRACTICE

We believe that the process of surveying current reading instruction practice is central to the creation of an action agenda and positive change in elementary school reading. In Part III of this book we examined the nature of one such examination, the replication of *The First R* study. The array of participants' answers describes the state of reading instruction and thousands of teachers who adopt eclectic approaches to helping their students become better readers. We believe that *The First R* questions themselves can help in the process of teachers' reflection on their work. The questions provide an opportunity to inventory instructional practice. The questions also are helpful in painting a portrait of teachers' and administrators' perceptions of practice.

The series of questions that we used to replicate *The First R* survey may serve as a useful model for the questions that are asked about current reading programs and instructional processes in a classroom, a school, or a district. They may help generate a self-examination of current practice. For example, *The First R* survey includes two groups of questions entitled "Organizing for Instruction" and "Accommodating Gifted and Struggling Readers." The first group of questions focuses on flexible grouping, individualized activity, the self-contained classroom, and ability grouping. The second group of questions focuses on how diverse readers are accommodated, the effectiveness of the instruction the readers receive, and the status of pull-out programs for particular readers. The questions serve as a menu of possible areas of inquiry, reflection, discussion, and possible change for teachers. They can provide initial guidance for teachers' and administrators' development of an action agenda. The questions may assist groups of interested teachers and administrators in an accounting of current practice and program in which issues of grouping and meeting individual students' needs are high priorities. A result may be the establishment of teacher inquiry around grouping issues, and a consultation of the rich research literature related to grouping. This consultation leads to focused inquiry on variations of cooperative grouping[13] within individual teachers' classrooms.

Improvement of reading programs requires clear understanding of what works and what does not work, and of the students whose needs are being met and those whose are not. Focused questions, such as those in the replication of *The First R*, help us collect this information. We believe that asking questions about practice also can serve other important causes. Questions that encourage the appraisal of the status quo also provide an opportunity to assess the precedent for reflective inquiry within a particular school or district. Initiating reflective inquiry in a particular school may be as difficult as positively changing reading instruction, but asking questions may help us better understand this reality. Asking questions may also allow for determination of the degree of inclusion of all school community stakeholders, and the nature and quality of the communication system that is necessary to discuss and inform reading program change. This careful accounting of practice should describe challenges and strengths of reading programs. Indeed, a positive occurrence in many schools and classrooms is that teachers are involved in framing research issues and in designing research studies and inquiry.

## CHARACTERISTICS OF SUCCESSFUL SCHOOLS

We examined aspects of engaged student readers and the nature of current elementary reading practice in Parts II and III of this volume. We arrive at this point with a new understanding of how teachers, administrators, and district personnel are approaching the challenge of teaching elementary students to read. This new understanding is complemented with the summary of recent research that describes effective elementary reading instruction. A result of this exercise is the determination that there is considerable research evidence to support particular reading instruction practices. Many teachers and many schools are providing the types of instructional materials and procedures that should help their students continue to develop into independent and successful readers. We want to acknowledge that for all the information gathered in our replication of *The First R* study, we do not have data that tell us that one approach to teaching reading is more effective than another. We cannot hang the hat of success on one particular description of effective curriculum and instruction. In fact, we are convinced that such an approach is unwise and futile. We can report that the majority of teachers and administrators who participated in the replication of *The First R* describe eclectic approaches to reading instruction that are molded to the perceived strengths and needs of individual students and classes.

The diverse individual characteristics of student readers in a classroom are often paralleled by the idiosyncratic nature of schools. Classrooms within schools and schools within districts and states have particular strengths and needs. There is no "one size fits all" program for improving reading performance in elementary schools, or for creating a community of engaged, dedicated professionals. What works varies. It is not the simple application of research findings that makes a successful reading program. The replication of an instructional approach that is successful in one school should not be the goal of another school. Rather, the focus should be on the establishment of a process that allows for determining needs and strengths of students, teachers, and schools. Furthermore, the process should be accompanied by resources to develop a reading program that addresses the strengths and needs, and contributes to positive change. The wealth of research information, whether created inside or outside a particular classroom and school,[14] needs to be married to emerging understanding of effective schools, to mechanisms for implementing positive school change, and to teachers' professional development.

Effective change occurs in environments that encourage and support the change process. Although we are reluctant to suggest *the* single profile of an effective elementary reading instruction program, we believe that reading programs thrive in schools that share common attributes. A detailed catalog of all that is occurring in school change literature is beyond the scope of this volume. Interested readers can consult the rich literature that examines successful school change programs. This includes reading-specific accounts of urban schools with economically disadvantaged student populations,[15] schools in which reading and writing are central to student success,[16] schools which invite and honor parent and family participation,[17] and schools with predominantly language-minority children.[18] This literacy-centered work is complemented by the more broad literature of school change.[19]

In total, the school change literature describes the shared characteristics of effective schools and instructional programs. These include effective leadership and clear commitment to excellence, adequate resources and ongoing support, an appropriate time frame for change, ongoing reflection and evaluation of programs, inclusion of diverse perspectives on reading and the change process, collaboration with school community members, and the effective communication of reading program materials, procedures, and goals. Each of these characteristics is vital to the establishment of a school environment that encourages and facilitates change, and each can impact the others.

Effective schools have clear leadership and a shared commitment to excellence. Throughout the change process, participants understand that the assumption of leadership by an individual or small group is assumed for the common good. Teachers and administrators who believe that their values are reflected in school goals and the paths to achieving these goals will defer to representative leadership. Leadership is assumed by school community members who are experts: experts in conceptualizing change, in facilitating change, and in building good will through the change process. Because expertise is determined by the needs of a particular school program, leadership should come from those best equipped to provide the expertise. This means that school change will tap the expertise of administrators, teachers, and parents.

Successful schools have adequate resources and support. Time and money are two key resources. Effective schools work within the parameters created by limits of resources, and they strive to increase resources. Support for teachers and schools is provided from district and central offices, with a concentration of fiscal resources beyond minimal amounts. Building administrators build on the central office support through their local decisions related to resource allocation and scheduling. Support from the school community is encouraged and used judiciously. Beyond physical resources, successful schools create and sustain a spirit that nurtures and motivates.

Successful schools undertake change efforts within an appropriate time frame. An effective reading program must be discussed, conceptualized, constructed, implemented, evaluated, and reflected on. Refinement of the vision and reality of the reading program should occur at each of these steps. Long-term solutions for persistent instructional challenges demand realistic time frames. If a school agrees that positive change is the result of ongoing reflection and refinement, then the time frame shifts to parallel the life of the school. Lasting and positive change most often takes time. Hence, the admonition to "make haste slowly."

Successful schools and teachers engage in the regular and ongoing examination and reflection of professional practice. Reflection is individual as teachers and administrators examine their work in relation to school goals and personal agendas for successful teaching. The reflection is also communal, as teachers and administrators consult their strategic plans and one another to determine if and how the school vision is being realized. The result of examination and reflection is renewed understanding of the work to be done, and the challenges that have been met.

Successful schools are inclusive and they invite collaboration and community involvement. Such schools believe that needs and strengths are best identified through collaborative efforts that engage all stakeholders within the school community. There is the shared belief that different kinds of expertise reside in different areas of school communities, and that these sources of expertise must be tapped. The sources of expertise within a school community might be part of family and community involvement in children's learning to read, parents and neighbors who bring funds of knowledge to classrooms, reflective teachers who best know their students and their practice, and administrators and teachers who are both instructional and spiritual leaders.

Successful schools develop effective communication systems. Any and all meaningful change in reading instruction must be anticipated and guided by clear communication among school community members. Efficient communication encourages the contributions of school community members, educates the public in relation to school goals and means, and it tells the stories of challenge and success. Communication allows interested school community members to know the workings of the school, be they parents, employers, or legislators. In short, we can expect that effective reading programs will evolve and thrive in ideal school environments. We may encapsulate this notion of the ideal school environment with the term *connectedness*.[20] People, programs, and plans for change are connected through the commitment of available resources and shared decision-making processes. Guiding these efforts is a school vision that contributes to a identifiable and engaging culture of place.[21]

## SUCCESSFUL READING PROGRAMS
## AND ONGOING PROFESSIONAL DEVELOPMENT

The previous sections of this part provide a preview of sorts, a preview of the content and process (specifically, knowledge and reflection) that are necessary to embark on an effective action agenda for positive change. In addition to the characteristics discussed in the previous section, successful schools and successful teachers share a particular habit of mind: They regularly seek to improve themselves through careful reflection. The checkered history of instructional change initiatives yields one consistent finding: a quality reading program is not comprised solely of good instructional materials and procedures. Rather, successful programs are realized when they are in the minds and hands of motivated and talented teachers, supported by administrators, parents, and community. Professional development is critical for the ongoing personal and professional growth of teachers and their reading instruction. Thus, it is imperative to meld reading program development with teachers' professional development.

Elmore, Peterson, and McCarthey[22] outlined aspects of professional development that contribute to superior instructional programs. They endorsed the establishment and maintenance of a professional culture that provides time and other resources so that teachers may interact and engage in sustained conversations that are relevant to their practice and their students. They noted that it is more than the implementation of a particular reading program and philosophy that makes for successful student readers. Teachers need to establish connections to professional communities, and to carry on personal and collaborative inquiry related to what their students most need. Elmore, Peterson, and McCarthey also described possible obstacles to change in teachers' work. These relate to teachers' immovable ideas about content and pedagogy, and the lack of experiences that might help teachers develop new knowledge about content and pedagogy. For example, a teacher who believes that children will learn to read by listening to other children may be content to read aloud to children on a daily basis. Similarly, a teacher who believes that instruction in phonemic awareness is all that children need to succeed as readers may provide daily skill and drill instruction. The value of teacher inquiry and discussion here is obvious: Whether the inquiry is conducted inside or outside a particular classroom, discussion around that inquiry may provide the evidence and alternative perspective that encourages reflection and convinces teachers to modify (and others to maintain) practice.

We noted earlier that we cannot attribute success to any of the many iterations of reading instruction recorded in our modified replication of *The First R* survey. There is an ongoing need for the local (i.e., classroom or school level) examination of the relationship between teachers' professional development and their students' achievement. However, one study has examined the relationship of particular professional development initiatives for reading teachers and the reading achievement of their students.[23] This study found positive and significant differences in the reading test scores of students whose teachers participate in professional development activities, when the professional development provides teachers the opportunity to examine their knowledge and practice, and to experience new thinking and approaches related to instruction. Based on her findings, Stallings suggested that teachers reflect on the current state of their instruction and student learning. This self-analysis can help teachers become aware of the need for improvement and change. It may also help teachers commit to change and create specific goals, such as exploring students' individual differences and attempting to optimize reading instruction for all students. Next, teachers can develop instruction that is informed by research and evaluate the effect of the research. Teachers may also observe each other's classrooms and analyze their own practice. This is accompanied by group discussions of successes and challenges related to students and their reading. Stallings found that these groups need and use a wide variety of approaches to professional development including examination of teaching models and teaching simulations, peer observations, and the critiquing of colleagues' practice.

The importance of professional development cannot be understated. Teachers who are given the privileges and responsibilities to reflect on current practice and to maintain successful practice or improve other practice will generally be more effective in the teaching of reading. The foundations of teachers' professional development include learning by doing (e.g., trying a word wall exercise for the first time), linking prior knowledge to new information (e.g., using professional knowledge of grouping to examine and critique student peer grouping practice and its effects), learning by identifying and reflecting on problems (e.g., participating in a collaborative teacher inquiry group on classroom-based reading assessment), and learning in a supportive environment (e.g., risk taking as teachers move from a familiar and comfortable reading program to one that is both challenging and promising). A caveat is necessary: If we read between the lines, we see that there are dollar signs and blocks of time that are necessary for teachers to experience and make the most of such professional development efforts.

## STRATEGIES FOR READING PROGRAM CHANGE: EXAMPLES FROM THE FIELD

In this section we focus on the strategic change of reading programs. We choose examples that combine strategic change and professional development, including teacher inquiry and research, reading program and reading assessment development, teacher book clubs, and the practice of teacher mentoring.

### Teacher Inquiry

Teacher inquiry allows for a focus on issues that influence classroom practice. When teachers develop inquiry-based projects and understandings that focus on their classrooms, the knowledge constructed may have more immediate application to student readers in their classrooms. We believe that it is vital (but not enough) to know the reading research literature, for, although it is important, it cannot by itself create positive change. Careful attention must be paid to the means by which knowledge is constructed by teachers, and how reading research information is used by teachers.[24] Resources not committed to encouraging teachers' construction of knowledge of locally important issues and challenges in reading may prevent positive school change.

Existing cases of teacher inquiry are rich and varied. Examples of teacher inquiry can be found in volumes dedicated to describing and encouraging teacher researchers.[25] Book length accounts of teacher research describe both the means and goals of inquiry, and teacher research method and focus. For example, we learn of the vitality of reading and writing instruction when the content and process of literacy truly connects with students lives, as when poetry writing taps adolescents' emotions and needs. We also learn of the value of one teacher's regular and meaningful reflection.[26] Teacher inquiry can also involve groups of teachers and researchers, as demonstrated by a project that focuses on teacher questions and student responses.[27] This collaboration is marked by teachers' shared concerns for perceived weaknesses in minority students' responses to teachers' questions. Teachers seek support from university researchers, and the ensuing inquiry results in new understandings of classroom discourse, individual student differences, and the roles that both teacher and university researcher can take in classroom inquiry. A second example of classroom teacher/university researcher collaboration examines changes in students' motivations and strategies within a literature-based science program.[28] Elementary classroom teachers and university researchers combine efforts to examine how concept-oriented reading instruction contributes to students' reading engagement, which was evidenced by changes in reading strategies and intrinsic motivation.

We are convinced that teacher inquiry is superior to the trickle-down model of reading research knowledge dissemination. By this, we mean reading research that is produced by university researchers without the collaboration of teachers, administrators, and students, and without concerted effort to disseminate potentially useful information to classroom teachers. Much research that might make a difference collects dust because the research results do not get into the minds and hands of teachers and administrators. Often, the reading research agenda is set by researchers who are not teachers. This presents several challenges. First, the research may not focus on the immediate, specific issues that the classroom teacher wants to examine. Second, even if there is congruence between researchers' program of investigation and a classroom teacher's needs, there may be no procedure or resources to translate the research and findings to information that is useable in the classroom. Third, it may be the case that a classroom teacher is not happy with a status quo that supports the funding and conducting of research by others outside the classroom. At the same time, teachers may not have the training to conduct research that yields high confidence results to fuel reading program change. New forms of teacher professional development demand that colleagues in higher education learn what may be new roles. University researchers who learn the role of collaborator, who model how research is conceptualized and designed (and who may learn aspects of this from teachers), and who serve as an expert resource on literature related to the focus of inquiry related to reading and instruction may have the greatest positive influence.

## Reading Assessment Programs

Reading assessment programs and teacher professional development is one area that is particularly rich with stories of success.[29] Each of these projects involves teachers who use professional prerogative to identify reading assessment practice that is in need of change, to gain approval and support for their action agenda, and to develop new visions and practice related to classroom, school, and district reading assessments. These teacher-initiated assessment projects focus on measuring the complexities of learning to read, and each receives support at the district and building levels that is critical for success. The successful undertaking of these projects represents concerted teacher professional development opportunity and accomplishment. The teachers' shared discussions of assessment necessarily focus on both school and individual teachers' values and goals. Thus, they engage critical aspects of positive school change, including communication and consensus building.

As an example, classroom teachers in Austin, Texas, developed The Primary Assessment of Language Arts and Mathematics (PALM),[30] in collaboration with researchers at the University of Texas. The PALM was developed in response to the districtwide use of the Iowa Test of Basic Skills to monitor elementary school quality. Teachers questioned whether the Iowa Test of Basic Skills was an appropriate measure of young students' reading ability, and they petitioned the Board of Trustees of the Austin Independent School District for the responsibility and opportunity to develop a more suitable reading assessment. The Board of Trustees granted teachers a waiver from the required standardized testing of first graders. In place, the charge of developing a more appropriate early literacy assessment was given to the teachers. The PALM was developed with the goal of providing useful assessment information for teachers, parents, administrators, policy makers, and students. The PALM goals statement was communicated to first-grade teachers in the district, and their participation was invited. The PALM team then created a reading development profile that describes characteristics and behaviors related to students' emergent reading, early reading, fluent reading, and expanding reading abilities. The reading development profile benefited from a piloting and refinement process that was inclusive and communicative, and supportive of teacher thinking and initiative. We believe that the process that led to the creation of the PALM is an exemplary model for programs that seek to combine program development with teachers' professional development.

Au[31] and Valencia and Place[32] also describe reading assessment program development that contributes to the growth of student readers while providing professional development opportunities for their teachers. Valencia and Place[33] sketch the development of The Bellevue Literacy Assessment Project.

Teachers in the Bellevue project were given time to meet and discuss their goals and values, and they created instructional outcomes and assessment materials and procedures that reflected current and shared understanding of reading and literacy. This portfolio project received support from parents and administrators, who charged teachers with developing an assessment program that met needs for accountability and for providing details of student learning. The assessment project allowed for the development and use of assessments that provided information for improving instruction, increasing student ownership of learning, and reporting accomplishments and challenges to stakeholders outside the classroom. The portfolio in Grade 1 was used to collect information on students' written retellings of stories, and their reading logs, free writing, and book reports. Similarly, Au[34] describes a comprehensive early literacy portfolio assessment program that was developed by teachers and administrators at the Kamehameha Early Education Project. The assessment program is tailored to the needs of students, teachers, administrators, and parents. It utilizes running records to determine students' word reading strategies, and samples of student writing to assess student reading comprehension and vocabulary knowledge. Students' responses to literature that is read aloud by teachers or read by the students themselves are also a focus of the assessment program.

An encouraging picture emerges from these reading assessment development efforts: it describes teachers who are central in the conceptualization and realization of useful school materials and practices. For example, teachers needed a deep and abiding knowledge of portfolio assessment and running records to meet with success in the new assessment program. The projects also demonstrate that the taking on of such important projects is fertile ground for continued professional development. The projects demand a solid knowledge base with grounding in classrooms and schools, and the relevant research literature. The projects also require ongoing reflection and discussion by all team members. These recent examples of reading assessment development may inform systemic reading program change and professional development efforts, as they provide details related to gaining support for an action agenda. Both the Austin and Kamehameha projects resulted from the determination that the status quo needed change, lobbying for reform, and developing, piloting, and refining educational materials and practices. All these are enhanced by the effective communication of information among stakeholders that invites participation, seeks inclusion, and in doing so, garners broad support.

## Teacher Bookclubs

Book clubs provide a forum for teachers to discuss shared readings in relation to the teachers' immediate practical and theoretical issues. As such, they work at the interface of reading program change and teacher professional development. For example, Flood, Lapp, Alvarez, Romero, Ranck-Buhr, Moore, Jones, Kabildis, and Lundgren[35] describe book clubs in which teachers and preservice teachers in ethnically diverse schools read and discussed books written by authors of African-American, Asian-American, European-American, or Mexican-American heritage. Teachers report several benefits from participating in the regular book club discussion sessions. First, the teachers learn about cultures other than their own, cultures from which their diverse student population come. The teachers report that they find this information useful in planning classroom instruction for the diversity of students in their classrooms. Participating teachers also report that they develop better understanding of their own literacy skills and teaching skills. That is, through regular discussions of their reading, the teachers develop sensitivity to the nature of their own reading and interpretive processes. They also better understand their speaking and listening skills and strategies, as they are used in the book club discussion sessions. Third, teachers report that they use their fellow participants' insights to enrich their own understandings of the books and the people inhabiting them, and report greater understanding and sensitivity to multicultural issues. A final benefit of the book clubs is that teachers are encouraged to reflect on issues in their ongoing professional development. For example, reflection on the processes used in book club discussions could help teachers focus on the nature of conversation and discussion about books. This focus might then serve as a point of departure for individual teachers to examine their own teaching and use of literature in their classrooms. Through this examination, teachers might decide to initiate particular discussion routines with students, to model specific question asking strategies, or to encourage students to construct literary understandings in accordance with their own prior knowledge and experience.

## Mentoring Excellence

Effective reading instruction practice can be informed by the professional development practice of mentoring. Many of us can point to mentoring relationships in which we were beneficiaries of expert advice, modeling, and discussion around the teaching of reading. Mentoring, when done well, can provide novice and experienced teachers with opportunities to further develop their teaching of reading ability. Successful mentoring helps teachers move from current levels of knowledge and ability to new levels of practice. Mentoring is a potentially powerful strategy for school and reading program improvement, but it faces a two-part challenge.[36] That is, mentoring requires that teachers assume roles and responsibilities with which many are not familiar. There may be few or no precedents for mentoring in particular schools. Furthermore, mentoring is demanding of time. Mentor teachers must be motivated and rewarded for the good work they do.

The potential role of mentoring in teachers' professional development is described by Sipe and McCarrier.[37] The authors believe that mentoring can provide the opportunity for teachers to better understand the social nature of learning. The mentor–mentee relationship highlights learning in a social setting. Furthermore, mentoring can provide teachers with scaffolded support that allows mentors to help mentees move through zones of proximal development from a current ability to a more sophisticated or complex ability. For example, a promising first-year teacher may work with a mentor teacher to conceptualize different approaches to grouping for reading instruction and meeting the needs of diverse students within the same classroom. The mentor can identify the mentee's current levels of knowledge and ability related to teaching different types of student, and help design lesson planning and teaching opportunities that build on this current knowledge and that represent a comfortable challenge to the mentee. Through feedback and ongoing support, the mentor teacher may help the first year teacher accomplish goals related to providing appropriate instruction to diverse groups of readers. Mentoring can assume several forms, from a transmission of tried and true practice to the symbiotic relationship that might develop between a seasoned veteran who is entrenched in a single successful practice and a novice teacher who brings new and promising ideas that are yet untested. The importance of the reciprocity between teachers' professional development and school reading program improvement cannot be understated. What is replenishing for teachers will not be supported unless it has a spillover effect on student performance.

## AN ACTION PLAN FOR STRATEGIC CHANGE

We arrive at this point convinced that effective reading programs are those that are informed by what research tells us about accomplished reading, effective reading instruction, and successful school change. Similarly, teachers' and administrators' knowledge and reflection serve as a sounding board for school efforts to examine current practice and consider the changes that may be needed. We believe that reading program change is best achieved through the familiar metaphor of engagement. Just as engaged readers are strategic, motivated, knowledgeable, and socially oriented, a successful reading program is characterized by teachers who are engaged in examining and bettering their instruction, administrators who are engaged in developing support systems, parents who are engaged in their children's learning, students who are engaged in their work, and school communities that are engaged in supporting both reading program refinement and teacher professional development. This challenging work must be situated in a resource-rich environment. We note that the characteristics of successful schools serve as enablers of effective action plans. Without certain characteristics, such as community involvement and clear communication, an action plan will face serious threats to success. A school environment that is lacking in the enabling factors described elsewhere in this chapter needs change, as does the targeted reading program.

We now present guidelines that can be used to help in the development and evaluation of effective reading programs. As is true with much of our learning and achievement, models and detailed explanations contribute to our constructing useful knowledge. We believe the following guidelines are suitably detailed, while retaining a general applicability for schools that are considering reading program change and that are seeking advice on the path to this change. The guidelines are the result of work to foster reading program improvement.[38] The guidelines focus on examining and evaluating the current reading program, engaging in collaborative dialog to create, maintain, or change aspects of the program, and developing and undertaking an action plan for change. In essence, the guidelines may enable a school (or school district, or group of teachers) to enact and refine reading programs using a seven-step process. This process serves as the dynamic foundation for program improvement in reading. The seven steps are:

1. Establishing priorities and mobilizing resources,
2. Setting the ground rules,
3. Describing the program GAPS,
4. Identifying needs,
5. Selecting and implementing strategies for change,
6. Monitoring and supporting change,
7. Evaluating and reflecting on growth.

We describe each of these steps in terms of its purpose and process. These descriptions are intentionally brief. We believe that the change process is greatly influenced by the contextual factors that define the schools and classrooms in which we work. Thus, the steps are intended to be universal to accommodate the particular people and social dynamics that are unique to each school. The steps should be taken in the order described. It is probable that some steps are more difficult than others, depending on the enabling characteristics of your school. Some steps may already be accomplished related to your particular school and school district. For example, a school improvement team may have determined that children need experiences with a wide variety of books. We expect that schools could use a variety of approaches to the seven steps. The crucial point is that the spirit of each of the seven steps should be addressed in the reading program reform effort, for this brings us closer to planning an action agenda to effect meaningful change.

## Establishing Priorities and Mobilizing Resources

Efforts to change reading programs are successful when they rest on a strong foundation. Each day there are many forces competing for our attention and our resources. We believe that the school administration must give a strong endorsement to the reading program by making it a clear priority and by providing firm resources. Teachers, parents, students, and school community members can help administrators understand the need to prioritize reading program change. Beyond the allocation of resources, it is important that administrators participate in the change process themselves, as instructional leaders and providers of support and resources. The dedication of resources should be accompanied by the determination of a leadership team to beneficially control the reading program change effort. The leadership team should be representative of the diversity of the education community, reflecting the perspectives of all stakeholders who are concerned with young children's reading development. We recommend that the leadership team be comprised of the smallest number of members that can adequately represent the diversity of stakeholders. Often, a team of 3 to 5 members is effective because it meets the criteria of representativeness and it is small enough to meet theoretical and practical challenges of major change. These range from determination of the constructs of reading and literacy that underlie programmatic change efforts to the scheduling of regular meetings that all team members can attend, respectively.

The leadership team must clearly establish and communicate the goal and nature of reform. The goodwill related to this effort will yield valuable dividends. Reading reform must be identified and embraced as the priority for change in the school. The commitment to reform must be complete from all the faculty and staff, and each member must have a well-defined role in the change process. In addition, a time-line for change must be established. Reading reform takes time, but planning carefully and setting both short-term and long-term goals can keep progress on track. Timelines help communicate long-term plans and the quality of the thinking and planning that undergirds successful reform efforts.

Public statements and public displays, including presentations, regularly scheduled memos, charts, and posters, should be used to announce the priorities for reading reform and to suggest the means to achieving priorities. How we communicate the image of reform is related to building awareness and support for the change effort. For example, the establishment of a feedforward system is important. As opposed to feedback, feedforward provides information from stakeholders that allows a degree of proactivity in planning and undertaking major school challenges. Feedforward can help guarantee that the voices of diverse members of the school community are heard in the process of planning and enacting change. We encourage you to involve parents, the community, and resource teachers as part of the effort. A system that engages the school community and encourages participation from different members of the community will fair better. In school and out of school, there are resources that can be marshaled to help the change effort: the parent who helps build school and classroom websites, the merchant who joins in a class literacy project, the retiree who tutors young readers each week, and the grandparents who work to embellish the content and learning that their children experience in school. We end this section with an important note: Resources as diverse as paper, a photocopier, logistical support, release time, and coffee and tea must be provided to support the effort.

## Setting the Ground Rules

Change often involves conflict. The provision of ground rules in an action plan for provides a means to achieving the often elusive goal of change. Thus, it is important that basic ground rules promote and protect the voicing of individual concerns as we embark on a program improvement effort. The inclusion of stakeholders involves the casting of a broad net, which leads to the harvesting of diverse values and beliefs related to literacy and reading. Ground rules provide a forum for each participant to voice and share their values and beliefs and to better understand others' values and beliefs. The goal is to create a reading program that is well-structured but flexible. Such a program offers opportunity and encouragement for differences in both philosophy and pedagogy. At the same time, the program must maintain the focus on the betterment of student and teacher experience and achievement. All efforts and energy are in the direction of attainment of the goal of a program that is dynamic and flexible, and that reflects the collective wisdom of the school community.

There are several ground rules we endorse for literacy program change. These may be tried and adapted as they meet a particular school's needs.

1.   All conversations and meetings related to literacy program improvement will be open to all who wish to attend and participate. Exclusion breeds ill will, so sunshine laws are appropriate: All of the important work of the action plan team should be accessible to the public.

2.   Decisions will be made on consensus and not on a vote with the majority ruling. In our experience, it is sometimes difficult to reach consensus. An issue as important as reading will have correspondingly strong beliefs. The end result of consensus building is broad representation of stakeholders and more strong commitment by the school community. It is not unreasonable to equate this process with jury deliberation: It is intellectually and emotionally challenging. It yields a consensus position in which each legitimate stakeholder feels represented and from which each member can participate in a position of power. The discussion and sharing of different possible paths to shared goals that occur during consensus building can enrich every member. An inclusive process that leads to consensus goals increases the chance that more people will embrace the effort.

3.   The professional decision-making responsibilities of individual teachers will not be compromised or threatened in the redesign of the program. Individual teachers must assume responsibility for their instructional decisions. The literacy program effort should not restrict options, but should provide a supportive context for accommodating individual approaches and differences in good teaching. For example, the building-wide goal of improving classroom libraries is an effort that should be informed by individual teachers' knowledge of their students' interests, strengths, and needs. Professional development opportunities should be available for those teachers and administrators who see the literacy program development effort as an avenue to further their professional growth and expertise.

4.   The goal for the program is that all students will be challenged to achieve at their maximum level of potential in reading. All decisions made in the action plan process must be aligned with this goal. All decisions must have

a clear (if sometimes indirect) connection to maximizing individual student achievement.

## Describing the GAPS: Goals, Activities, Products, and Standards

Reading programs are directed toward particular Goals (G). Activities (A) are crafted to provide students and teachers with contexts for reading instruction, practice, and assessment. Each of these activities is directed toward these Goals. The Products (P) of these activities are student and teacher learning and growth, broadly defined to include both the cognitive and affective outcomes that are the hallmark of a successful reading programs. Standards (S) are applied to judge the quality of the goals, activities, and teaching and learning that are part of the reading program.

Describing the Goals, Activities, Products, and Standards of a reading program is an important early step in a reading program improvement process. Unfortunately, this step is often overlooked. There may be the tempting but dangerous practice of moving too quickly to address perceived needs for change without careful consideration and documentation of the current program. Securing an accurate description of the existing program involves the collection, analysis and interpretation of a great deal of data, but self-examination of the existing program is helpful in several ways. The result of this self-examination is the description of current reading instructional methods and materials, assessment processes and items, and the congruence of methods and materials with goals, beliefs, and values. Perceived needs should be checked against actual needs, as determined in the consensus building process.

Some of the data that help answer the question "What is our reading program like?" may already exist. For example, there may be reading program practice surveys conducted by the school parent–teacher organization, accounts of school reading program in relation to state guidelines and standards, or a narrative self-study. Whatever the existing store of information, it is almost certain that more information will need to be collected. Tools and strategies for collecting this information should be created locally. The data gathering process may not always be straightforward. For example, teachers may not be comfortable describing how the materials that they must use are in opposition to the things they value. Parents may not agree with the nature of the reform effort's decision-making processes, and they may find it difficult to openly describe their displeasure. It is critical to anticipate such situations, and to work diligently to alleviate them. An open forum and the establishment of trust between members of the effort will encourage discussion and debate. Members must always understand that while there may individual differences in how problems are conceptualized and how they are solved, there is shared effort toward reaching common goals.

One approach would be to take the nine principles outlined in Part II and use these as the framework for collecting data. Consider Instructional Principle 3 (p. 33):

*Effective reading instruction encourages students to become skilled in ways to adapt their reading strategies to their purposes and to text characteristics.*

Using this statement as a benchmark, members of a leadership team could examine curricular materials, practices, and goals to determine if the existing program can help students further develop their reading skills and strategies. The following might then help focus on the alignment between the proposed change and current practice:

Goals:        To what degree does this principle reflect a goal in our read-
              ing program?

Activities:   What array of learning activities do we offer our students to
              support this principle?

Products:     What evidence do we have of teacher professional develop-
              ment and student learning related to this principle?

Standards:    How do the data we have collected on student learning in
              this area hold up in comparison to recognized norms?

A second option is to begin with an existing document (if one exists) that describes the current program in terms of its critical features. Such an existing curriculum framework may describe a vision of an effective reading curriculum that is thorough and consensus-built. This kind of document can be used to further clarify or determine the goals of the program. From this point, data can be collected on the current program as they relate to these goals. It may also be fruitful to consult school or district goals documents at this point. This allows the opportunity to examine the alignment of local goals with state and national agendas, and other influential documents and their related goals. The examination of existing curricular documents should occur with the knowledge that they may be outdated. They may be misaligned with current practice, or with current goals. The current program description may be appropriate, or lacking in relation to student diversity and the needs of individual students.

It may be the case that reading program documents are not helpful, or not available. Here, a third option is to begin with the development of a consensus statement that reflects: a definition of reading; the goals of the reading program delineated by type (e.g., decoding, comprehension, motivation, affective interaction); and level (e.g., primary or intermediate grades). The activities, products, and standards for each of these goals areas are then developed and described. Which ever path is followed, the process is intended to be descriptive, not evaluative. The goal is to represent and articulate the program as it exists, not how it might be or what it was intended to be. A document should emerge from this process, and all participants should agree that it reflects the current state of the program. It may be helpful to envision this consensus document as a matrix that links the Goal, Activities, Products, and Standards together.

In some cases the data that will support the writing of a GAPS description exist. In some cases new data will need to be collected. The new data may be gathered using teacher interviews or surveys. In some cases, there may be need to collect new data on specific student outcomes. These assessments may involve sampling strategies or they may involve setting up new systems for documenting activity (e.g., observation of students' interactions related to particular reading selections and tasks, checklists of types of reading encountered by students, the frequency of student's checking out books from the library). In any case, it is important to be creative in the approach to determining the types of data that best serve the consensus goals of the school community, and in determining the means by which data will be gathered.

## Identifying Needs

This step involves the careful analysis of the existing program and determination of any discrepancies between the reality of the existing program and the ideal vision contained in the GAPS document. Discrepancies may exist in different places within the current program. An obvious concern is discrepancy between student performance (products) and standards. For example, we may discover that the fluency levels for our primary-grade students are well below recognized norms for fluency. Or we may find that many students have a troubling lack of motivation as they read. There are other places to look for discrepancies. For example, there may be goals within the program that are not targeted with any instructional activities (e.g., How do we meet our goal of providing increasingly diverse reading experiences for our students with our limited library resources?). There may be activities that are not clearly tied to goals. There may be goals that are not monitored in relation to student outcomes. The product of Step 4 should be a listing of discrepancies within the program as a whole. The goal is to be exhaustive in the description of these discrepancies for they provide a blueprint of the work that is needed to connect instruction and learning to the consensus goals of the school.

## Selecting and Implementing Strategies for Change

In this step, priorities are set for reading program improvement. It is quite likely that there are more areas of need that have been identified than can possibly be addressed in the short-term. For example, identified areas of need may be increased ability to decode words, increased opportunity to experience the diversity of multicultural literature, and increased sensitivity to student readers' individual differences. We recommend working toward a consensus that targets areas of need that the group considers most important. It is appropriate to determine what goals might be reasonably expected to be met as the target areas are chosen. For example, if motivation is a consensus concern work can proceed with the task of developing instruction and learning activities that have emphasis on student motivation.

The first steps are designed to get the system up and working. Solving some of the little problems early in the change process may set the ground-work for successfully tackling the bigger more difficult challenges later. And initial success in the change process should prove motivating for team members. We advocate the rank-ordering by importance of the tasks to be done. This can clarify the types of resources that are needed for each of the tasks. This is difficult work, for there are often many parts of the whole that could use immediate attention. We believe it is better to address and attain a single goal than to address and fail at several goals. This is especially important if the context determines that initial success at changing the reading program is the contingency for follow-up funding and resources for the other important needs and goals.

We suggest that some of the strategies we outlined earlier in this part be considered as ways to get started in identifying specific program improvement efforts. These include teachers' action research of aspects of teaching and learning that are determined by consensus to be critical to school success, book clubs in which teachers read and discuss writing related to their prioritized goals, the mentoring provided by master teachers, and the development and refinement of curricular materials and activities. The goal is to develop a plan that addresses the established priorities. The priorities for change may be different at different levels within the program or even within interest groups. It is not necessary that everyone be working on exactly the same issue or problem area. It may be beneficial to work in subgroups based on interests, if the resources and leadership are present. Several different initiatives, that reflect some choices on the part of those participating, may be in order so long as they do not place an undue burden on the structure and resources of the change plan. In concluding this section, we note that the work of setting and implementing strategies for change can have two foci: work that changes and improves current instruction and learning, and work that contributes to the effective change process. In essence, this requires that we are metacognitive about the way we enact an action plan and that we are sensitive and alert to the means by which the action plan can be ever improved.

## Monitoring and Supporting Change

Implementation of a reading program action plan should be accompanied by procedures for monitoring the change process. It is important the changes in instruction be documented as well as strategies for monitoring student growth and learning. This contributes to the accountability of the reading program team members, and it may provide a model for future efforts by different teachers, administrators, and schools. For example, accounts of the work done in reading assessment development and reform by teachers in Texas,[39] Washington,[40] and Hawaii[41] may help other school communities better understand the nature of school reform, the optimal levels of effort and resources, and challenges and accomplishments. These accounts portray the importance of leadership that garners a broad base of support in the school community and encourages smooth group dynamics. The accounts also describe the important practice of anticipating checkpoints at which the progress of the action plan can be assessed. For example, conducting an adequate review of existing literature to determine that the construct of reading at the local school level is related to what research tells us about reading, and checking the links between developing instructional materials and procedures and the reading construct both contribute to maximizing the action plan effort.

The experience of others also demonstrates that new and more valid measures may be required by new constructs and goals of reading instruction. It is important to recognize that successful change requires not only a change in the existing practices, but also a willingness to adapt the plan for change itself based on what works and what does not. In other words, the plan for change that was targeted in Step 5 (Selecting and Implementing Strategies for Change) must be seen as tentative and flexible. Change the plan if need be. Do not become so wedded to an answer that you lose sight of the question that started the search. We note that this is not easy work. It is not automatic and it is similar to other complex sets of strategies, social interactions, and motivations: Time and effort are requisite, as is the ability to work with others while honoring their perspectives and experiences.

## Evaluating and Reflecting on Growth

As reading program change is discussed and initiated, the need for evaluation of both the program and program development process become more pronounced. The monitoring of program change process requires ongoing assessment. It is necessary to set a target for developing a plan that includes conducting periodic evaluations of the success of the program implementation or change effort. Assessment and evaluation need to be tied to consistent questions that might include: How has our program changed? To what degree have we been successful in meeting the GAPS in our program design?

Our experience is that meaningful and lasting change in reading programs is attained through the careful development and use of evaluation procedures and materials. Assessments must honor the new reading curriculum and the achievement of teachers and students. Without the good fit of assessment to the newly developed reading program goals, the evaluation system will not be sensitive to the good things that students and teachers accomplish, and this may raise questions about the value of the program. Certain school community members will want to know "What is this accomplishment in terms of a standardized, norm-referenced test?" Thus, part of the challenge of creating a convincing new reading program is to develop reliable, valid, and convincing measures of reading.

The diverse paths to reading program excellence share important characteristics, including those described earlier in this part. Successful school change efforts are marked by additional, critical features. First, action plans are given time to succeed. Positive change takes large amounts of time, effort, and resources. This cannot be stressed too strongly. Changes in curriculum materials and practices are most often contemplated, adopted, or created in response to immediate needs. The urgency of these situations may contribute to a timeline for development and implementation that is most often too short for the piloting and refinement phases that high quality curricular materials and practices demand. It is helpful to remember that many current school practices represent the product of thousands of hours of the development process. Innovative and effective curricular changes must be given sufficient time and funding to realize their full potential.

Second, successful change thrives in a supportive community. Both spiritual and material resources are needed to fuel the hard work, long hours, and critical thinking that must occur to effect positive change. Whereas money is certainly necessary, vision and commitment complete the equation that leads to reading program improvement. Support and broad expertise reside in all school communities. Successful reading programs tap the variety of expertise as it exists in the school community, and are guided by leadership that is knowledgeable, focussed, and representative of the diversity of perspectives on reading within a community.

A third general characteristic is that reading program excellence is informed both globally and locally. Relevant reading research is consulted or conducted for guidance in critical issues related to reading program change. Reflective practitioners regularly examine their own practice to inform future practice, creating a self-improving reading program. Such programs are marked by proactivity and reactivity. Teachers, administrators, and parents are able to anticipate future needs, challenges and successes, and to adjust resources and action plan focus accordingly. Successful programs also look back. Past accomplishments are a strong motivator, and surveying what has passed helps build the map that gives direction to future efforts.

## FINAL THOUGHTS

Constructing an effective school reading program can be the most challenging, emotional, intellectually stimulating, and rewarding task that a school undertakes. Hearts and minds must be engaged in school action plans for reading programs to fully develop and prosper. Melding reading research with an accounting of current reading program practices places schools in an excellent position to effect positive change in school reading programs. In turn, that change can contribute to students' increased reading achievement for in the 21st century. We hope that this volume has served the three major purposes established by the authors in our action plan for writing the book: to describe what we know about how children become engaged readers, to describe the current state of reading instruction, and to describe the characteristics of effective schools and reading program development.

We believe it is unfortunate that so much time and energy are spent on the seemingly endless debate about what approach to teaching reading is best. Too often, this debate leads to overzealous and underfunded initiatives that have small chance of achieving long-lasting and positive change. Clearly, the best approach to teaching reading is one that is determined through a careful process of examination of curriculum, students, community, and models of reading. Effective reading program change is influenced by teachers' reflection and self-examination related to their goals, their knowledge, and their plans to be exemplary teachers of reading. We reiterate our belief that the excellent school reading program cannot be found on a shelf. It is created in the workplaces of the school community: the teachers' lounge, the school auditorium, and teachers' and parents' kitchens and living rooms. Reading program excellence is created locally. Our hope is that this book informs the change process with which schools can go about the business of transforming practice. The challenge to teach reading well to all students is great. We believe this challenge is best considered an opportunity: an opportunity to engage in a creation process that models professionalism and accomplishment for our students, our colleagues, and our school communities. The result of this creative process is the reading program that is best for a particular school, the reading program that helps teachers and students fully realize the potential of the first r.

## NOTES

1. Williams, P., Reese, C., Campbell, J., Mazzeo, J., & Phillips, G. (1995). *1994 NAEP Reading: A first look*. Washington, DC: National Assessment of Educational Progress.
2. Heath, S. (1983). *Ways with words: Language, life, and words in communities and classrooms*. Cambridge, UK: Cambridge University Press.
3. Moll, L., Amanti, C., Neff, D., & Gonzalez, N. (1992). Funds of knowledge for teaching: Using a qualitative approach to connect homes and classrooms. *Theory Into Practice, 31*, 132–141.
4. Allington, R. (1980). Poor readers don't get to read much in reading groups. *Language Arts, 57*, 872–877.
5. Deci, E., & Ryan, R. (1991). A motivational approach to self: Integration in personality. In R. Dienstbier (Ed.), *Nebraska Symposium on Motivation: Vol. 38. Perspectives on motivation*. (pp. 199–236). Lincoln: University of Nebraska Press.
6. Goswami, U., & Bryant, P. (1990). *Phonological skills and learning to read*. Hillsdale, NJ: Lawrence Erlbaum Associates.
7. Pressley, M., & Afflerbach, P. (1995). *Verbal reports of reading: The nature of constructively responsive reading*. Mahwah, NJ: Lawrence Erlbaum Associates.
8. Rosenblatt, L. (1938). *The reader, the text, the poem*. Carbondale: Southern Illinois University Press.
9. Delpit, L. (1988). The silenced dialogue: Power and pedagogy in educating other people's children. *Harvard Educational Review, 58*, 280–298.
10. Shockley, B., Michalove, B., & Allen, J. (1995). *Engaging families: Connecting home and school literacy communities*. Portsmouth, NH: Heinemann.
11. Vygotsky, L. (1978). *Mind in society: The development of higher psychological processes*. Cambridge, MA: Harvard University Press.

12. Gambrell, L., & Almasi, J. (1996). *Lively discussions! Fostering engaged reading.* Newark, DE: International Reading Association.
13. Slavin, R. (1987). *Cooperative learning: Student teams* (2nd ed.). Washington, DC: National Education Association.
14. Cochran-Smith, M., & Lytle, S. (1990). Research on teaching and teacher research: The issues that divide. *Educational Researcher, 19,* 2–11.
15. Winfield, L. (1995). Change in urban schools with high concentrations of low-income children: Chapter 1 schoolwide projects. In R. Allington & S. Walmsley (Eds.) *No quick fix: Rethinking literacy programs in America's elementary schools* (pp. 214–235). New York: Teachers College Press.
16. Allington, R., & Cunningham, P. (1996). *Schools that work: Where all children read and write.* New York: Harper Collins.
    Atwell, N. (1998). *In the middle: New understandings about writing, reading, and learning* (2nd ed.). Portsmouth, NH: Heinemann.
17. Delgado-Gaitan, C. (1990). *Literacy for empowerment: The role of parents in children's education.* New York: The Falmer Press.
    Morrow, L. (1995). *Family literacy: Connections in schools and communities.* Newark, DE: International Reading Association.
18. Goldenberg, C., & Gallimore, R. (1991). Local knowledge, research knowledge, and educational change: A case study of first-grade Spanish reading improvement. *Educational Researcher, 20,* 2–14.
19. Barth, J. (1990). *Improving schools from within: Teachers, parents, and principals can make the difference.* San Francisco: Jossey-Bass.
    Fullan, M. (1993). *Change forces: Probing the depths of educational reform.* London: Falmer Press.
    Lieberman, A. (1995). *The work of restructuring schools: Building from the ground up.* New York: Teachers College Press.
    Murphy, J. (1991). *Restructuring schools: Capturing the phenomenon.* Beverly Hills, CA: Sage.
20. Wimpleberg, R. (1989). The dilemma of instructional leadership and a central role for the central office. In W. Greenfield (Ed.), *Instructional leadership: Concepts, issues, and controversies* (pp. 100–117). Boston: Allyn & Bacon.
21. Bruner, J. (1996). *The culture of education.* Cambridge, MA: Harvard University Press.
22. Elmore, R., Peterson, P., & McCarthey, S. (1995). *Restructuring in the classroom: Teaching, learning, and school organization.* San Francisco: Jossey-Bass.
23. Stallings, J. (1989, April). *School achievement effects and staff development: What are some critical factors?* Paper presented at the American Educational Research Association annual meeting, San Francisco.
24. Harste, J. (1993). Response to Ridgeway, Dunston, & Quian: Standards for instructional research. *Reading Research Quarterly, 28,* 356–358.
25. Gitlin, A., Bringhurst, K., Burns, M., Cooley, V., Myers, B., Price, K., Russell, R., & Tiess, P. (1992). *Teachers' voices for school change: An introduction to educative research.* New York: Teachers College Press.
    Hubbard, R., & Power, B. (1993). *The art of classroom inquiry: A handbook for teacher-researchers.* Portsmouth, NH: Heinemann.
26. Atwell, N. (1998). *In the middle: New understandings about writing, reading, and learning* (2nd ed.). Portsmouth, NH: Heinemann.
27. Edwards, B., & Davis, B. (1997). Learning from classroom questions and answers: Teachers' uncertainties about children's language. *Journal of Literacy Research, 29,* 471–505.

28. Guthrie, J., Van Meter, P., McCann, A., Wigfield, A., Bennett, L., Poundstone, C., Rice, M., Faibisch, F., Hunt, B., & Mitchell, A. (1996). *Growth of literacy engagement: Changes in motivation and strategies during concept-oriented reading instruction.* (Reading Reseach Report No. 53). Athens, GA: National Reading Research Center.
29. Au, K. (1994). Portfolio assessment: Experiences at the Kamehameha elementary education program. In S. Valencia, E. Hiebert & P. Afflerbach (Eds.), *Authentic assessment: Practices and possibilities* (pp. 103–126). Newark, DE: International Reading Association.
    Hoffman, J., Worthy, J., Roser, N., McKool, S., Rutherford, W., & Strecker, S. (1996). Performance assessment in first-grade classrooms: The PALM model. In D. Leu, C. Kinzer, & K. Hinchman (Eds.), *Literacies for the 21st century: Research and practice,* 100–112. Chicago: National Reading Conference.
    Valencia, S., & Place, N. (1994). Literacy portfolios for teaching, learning, and accountability: The Bellevue literacy assessment project. In S. Valencia, E. Hiebert, & P. Afflerbach (Eds.), *Authentic assessment: Practices and possibilities* (pp. 134–156). Newark, DE: International Reading Association.
30. Hoffman, J., Worthy, J., Roser, N., McKool, S., Rutherford, W., & Strecker, S. (1996). Performance assessment in first-grade classrooms: The PALM model. In D. Leu, C. Kinzer, & K. Hinchman (Eds.), *Literacies for the 21st century: Research and practice* (pp. 100–112). Chicago: National Reading Conference.
31. Au, K. (1994). Portfolio assessment: Experiences at the Kamehameha elementary education program. In S. Valencia, E. Hiebert, & P. Afflerbach (Eds.) *Authentic assessment: Practices and possibilities* (pp. 103–126). Newark, DE: International Reading Association.
32. Valencia, S., & Place, N. (1994). Literacy portfolios for teaching, learning, and accountability: The Bellevue literacy assessment project. In S. Valencia, E. Hiebert, & P. Afflerbach (Eds.), *Authentic assessment: Practices and possibilities* (pp. 134–156). Newark, DE: International Reading Association.
33. Valencia & Place, 1994.
34. Au, 1994.
35. Flood, J., Lapp, D., Alvarez, D., Romero, A., Ranck-Buhr, W., Moore, J., Jones, M., Kabildis, C., & Lundgren, L. (1994). *Teacher book clubs: A study of teachers' and student teachers' participation in contemporary multicultural fiction literature discussion groups.* (Research Report No. 22). Athens, GA: National Reading Research Center.
36. Little, J. (1990). The "mentor" phenomenon and the social organization of teaching. In C. Cazden (Ed.), *Review of research in education* (Vol. 16, pp. 297–351). Washington, DC: American Educational Research Association.
37. Sipe, L., & McCarrier, A. (1995). Constructing a knowledge base for in-school leadership in a schoolwide literacy model. In K. Hinchman, D. Leu, & C. Kinzer (Eds.), *Perspectives on literacy research and practice* (pp. 428–437). Chicago, IL: National Reading Conference.
38. Hoffman, J. (1998). *GAPS: A Discrepancy Evaluation Model for Reading Program Improvement.* Unpublished manuscript, University of Texas.
39. Hoffman, 1996.
40. Valencia & Place, 1994.
41. Au, 1994.

# Author Index

Note: An *italicized page number* means that a full citation to an author's work is located on that page.

# Subject Index

Note: *Italicized letters f* and *t* following page numbers refer, respectively, to figures and tables.

## A

Ability grouping, 61, 63*t*, 80
Activities, reading, 29–33, 37–39,
    52–54, 56, 94–96
Aesthetic experience, 27–29, 31, 33, 41,
    68–69
African-American students, 41
After Reading Activities, 37
Alphabetic principle, 6, 15–16, 19–20,
    30–31
Alphabetic writing, 1–2
Anthropological research, 77
Applying skills and strategies, 13–26,
    14*f*, 19*f*, 24*f*, 66–68, *see also*
    Skill development
Assessment, *see* Models, assessment;
    Performance assessment
Audio tapes, 22, 51
Austin, M. C.
    *The First R,* 59–65, 62*t*–64*t*
    *The Torchlighters,* 60
Austin Independent School District
    (Texas), 87–88
Automatic word recognition, 6, 13–19,
    23, 67
    code instruction for, 14–18
    decoding components of, 6, 13,
    18–19, 23

## B

Balanced reading, 4*f,* 7
    achieving goals for, 62*t,* 72–73
    Piaget and, 7, 72
    principles for, as practiced, 59–73
    principles for, in theory, 13–56
    principles vs. practice, 65–72, 66*t*
    support for, 8–9, 61
Before Reading Activities, 37
Bellevue Literacy Assessment Project,
    87–88
Benchmark Program, 18
"Big idea" issues, 40–41, 69
Book clubs, 31–33, 68–69, 88–89
Book formats, 22–23, 25–26, 30,
    41–46, 69–70

## C

Carnegie reading study, *see First R, The*
    (Austin and Morrison)
Challenges, 16, 36, 64*t, see also* Im-
    proving reading instruction
    literacy and, 2, 8–9, 11, 21–22,
    40–41
    student texts as, 19, 21–23, 39–40,
    46, 51, 60